THE GRAND CANADIAN
ROCKIES

THE GRAND CANADIAN
ROCKIES

TEXT AND PHOTOGRAPHS BY
GEORGE BRYBYCIN

GB PUBLISHING

INTRODUCTION

Some people may wonder whether a book's introduction should focus on the subject of the book or on the book itself. To be true to the subject and how the book presents it, perhaps both should be discussed.

The spectacular Rocky Mountains are the world's second longest mountain range, next to the Andes, and measure an impressive 1500 km with width ranging from 80 to 100 km. The backbone of the North American continent originates in the State of New Mexico in the southern USA, stretches north into Canada, and terminates at Liard River in northern British Columbia by the Yukon border. This volume presents the splendour of the Canadian Rockies only. Because of their northern latitude the Canadian Rockies portray more Alpine or Himalayan-like features. The tree line varies from 2500m in the south to 2100m in the north. Large icefields and glaciers are permanent and common at high elevations and are more prevalent on the north sides of mountains. The Rockies' ice and snow feed several large rivers, which flow to the Pacific, Atlantic and Arctic Oceans. A few of the largest rivers are: Columbia, Fraser, Liard, Peace, Athabasca, Sunwapta, Saskat-chewan and the Bow River. The monarch of the Canadian Rockies is monumental and challenging Mount Robson, which rises to a respectable elevation of 3953m. The other five tallest elevations are: Mt. Columbia (3747m), North Twin (3683m), Clemenceau (3657m), Alberta (3619m), and Assiniboine (3618m).

The climate can vary widely from south to north and east to west. Western regions of the Rockies are under Pacific influence where the climate is moist and warm. The east side features a dry continental climate. Winters are cold in the south, colder in the central part, and coldest in the far north, where minimum temperatures may reach -40°C or colder. Snowfall is at its maximum along, and west of, the Great Divide and moderate to low east of it. The Rockies are home to rich and diverse flora and fauna. High alpine meadows boast a spectacular showcase of mountain flowers, plants and shrubs. From early summer to autumn, the meadows teem with life, sounds and aromas. It is here that a variety of herbs with miraculous medicinal and health properties thrive. Birds nest here and rodents build their burrows. The most northern hemisphere species of fauna is prevalent here. Moose, Elk, Caribou, Deer, Goat, Sheep, Grizzly and Black Bear, are quite common throughout the Rockies. Large carnivores are also found here, such as, the Wolf, Coyote, Wolverine, Red Fox, Cougar, Lynx and Bobcat. The most prominent birds of prey or raptors are the Bald and Golden Eagles, Hawks, Falcons, Owls, and fish-eating Osprey. Other larger birds include the Raven, Crow, Magpie, Gray Jay, Clark's Nutcracker, Stellar's Jay, Blue Jay, Geese, and a variety of Ducks, including the Loon.

The Rocky Mountain forests, impressive in the past, are now decimated by indiscriminate clear cut logging, where entire areas were cut down causing landslides, erosion and floods, and completely destroying wildlife habitat. Only those areas protected by National Parks remain somewhat pristine. For this reason, we desperately need to enlarge and create new National Parks to give the Rockies maximum protection.

The author and designer of this 'creation' is a mountain man, naturalist and 'reasonable' environmentalist, who - don't tell anybody - hugs a tree or two occasionally. Therefore, this book presents the natural regions of the pristine Rockies. Hopefully, books such as this, will exert some influence – therefore the script and the photo selections represent a "don't abuse it or you will lose it" concept. The photographs feature the most beautiful parts of the Rockies and may trigger in the viewer's mind the idea of the need to respect and preserve. Who would want to destroy, or damage, such glorious beauty? Since the author is a staunch back-country explorer, the book also reflects that aspect: remote areas, high vistas, climbing, camping and bivouacking. Also included are photos of well-known landmarks, such as Lake Louise, Peyto or Mt. Robson which many of you may recognize, love and want to see again and again.

The saying goes 'everything at night is black'. Well, have a look. Night photography is widely represented here and you will discover that 'not all is black at night'. The author enjoys photographing at night because, although difficult, he enjoys the challenge it presents. The book also contains some so-called 'accidental' photos, where the photographer may have run into something or something may have run into the photographer; not much work but fast action and a lot of luck is involved.

The vertical book format lends itself well to large photos. The dilemma is how to give maximum justification to a panoramic view, which by nature is horizontal. This book design does not allow for the large size. Using double spread photos is very controversial because many book lovers complain that the photos are 'cut in half'. Also, when the photo is too large, it loses sharpness and colour quality, and becomes overwhelming. Therefore, many horizontal photos are cropped on both sides to have a squarer look, thus appearing larger. Many large art books feature full-page photos only, with captions at the back of the book. While that style may appear elegant and classy, it can also be annoying as you must search for the caption of each photo. There is also the wear and tear it certainly will cause to the book.

This book is intended to create a maximum of visually artistic and intellectual pleasures. Hopefully, it will touch and enrich your life in some ways, and arouse your awareness and need to protect and preserve our gorgeous, but very endangered and fast-vanishing, wilderness. Be a part of that beautiful concept of preserving our Rockies forever.

TALES OF THE HEIGHTS

As you browse through these pages, it will soon dawn on you that this is not material collected along the roadside in three months, or photographed from the air in five days. Here you see lifelong efforts of a mountain man who 'has seen most of it', from ground level, from the top of a mountain, from a high ridge, or remote high valley, during the day and at night, in summer and in winter, rain or shine.

You will glimpse at a ferocious Grizzly, a thunderstorm, a glorious sunrise, or mysterious moonlight. You will witness man's struggle to conquer the mountains; and then you will realize that the mountains will only occasionally allow or tolerate man's intrusion, but conquering is not really an option. The mountain will unleash its arsenal of weapons to punish and defeat a 'little' man, an intruder, who tries to disturb the proud majesty of the heights. Being curious and adventuresome as we are, danger and hardship only arouses and stimulates our passion for the mountains. That is why we climb, scramble or hike.

A long, long time ago, when I was young and a bit foolish, I decided to climb and bivouac on top of Mt. Worthington (2838m) in Kananaskis Country. How to get there? From upper Kananaskis Lake, a good trail leads west through lush forest and a valley to a steep headwall, beyond which nestles picturesque Three Isle Lake. A bit farther west, the trail reaches South Kananaskis Pass (2267m). Before reaching the Pass, I turned left (south) and scrambled through large boulders, scree, snow and some ice, toward Worthington-McHarg Col. It was early summer, the weather was unstable (windy and rainy) with the upper reaches all snowed in. Days were long, I was tired and wet. In those days, Gore-Tex and polypropylene were unknown. The rain and perspiration made me wetter and colder, worse yet, the temperature dropped to well below freezing. I made it close to the summit and, with some difficulty, set up my tent in a little gully, away from the hostile elements. I enjoyed my 'dinner' which consisted of an apple and a piece of chocolate, and quickly crawled into my half-wet down sleeping bag. Sleep would not come as I felt increasingly cold, then I began to shiver, shivering like I had never before experienced. Fully clothed I began 'exercising' inside of my sleeping bag to try to get my blood circulating, but nothing stopped my increased shivers. When my jaw started rattling loudly, I realized hypothermia had set in. A dry undershirt to change into would most likely save me, but all I had were the wet clothes I was wearing.

After a while, realizing my shivers were increasing, the thought of freezing to death crossed my mind. Then I remembered I had a small plastic bottle of brandy in my packsack. Still capable of thinking and reasoning, I knew that consuming alcohol in my situation could only aggravate my condition. On the other hand, unless I did some-thing drastic and fast, I might be dead in five minutes. Since the brandy was the only 'medicine' at hand, I decided to drink it. My 'frozen solid' hands could not unscrew the plastic cap on the bottle. Gripping the cap with my teeth didn't work either. Now my half frozen brain told me to put the bottle between my knees and try to unscrew the cap with my palms. It worked.

Without delay, I consumed 100 grams of potent brandy. My immediate reaction was one of hope and well-being. Being a non-drinker, the reaction was immediate and powerful. First, it felt like my stomach was on fire, then the fire went down to my feet, and soon my head was about to explode. Next came a foreign sensation, very relaxing, and my shivers disappeared. That's all I remember. Snore! snore!.

Upon awaking next morning, I was warm, rested, and ready, to face a full-sized blizzard. After a meager breakfast, I packed up my 'contraption' and quickly headed off into the unknown as the visibility neared zero. After 30 minutes of slipping and sliding, tumbling and falling, the blizzard and snow subsided and visibility improved considerably. Walking down was not great fun, but I made it back without any major disaster. The Grizzlies were no doubt snoring happily in their dens on a day like that. Smart Bears! For me, it was a hard lesson learned. To this day, it makes me wonder whether you would be reading this story if I didn't have the brandy.

We are told history often repeats itself. Sure enough, it recently almost did for me when I climbed Mt. Worthington in mid-October. That nearly tragic earlier trip produced no pictures due to the horrible weather. This time, I chose a dry spell and photography looked very promising. I approached from the South Col via South Ridge, but I made one small but costly, mistake. From Three Isle Lake, going southward, I wandered a bit too far before turning right (west). Result: I had to bushwhack through incredibly thick forest and extremely steep slopes, including surmounting some walls. All this took time and energy, so when I reached the South Col, the sun was sinking low. As I pushed towards the summit, darkness approached quickly, and unusually cold strong westerly winds hampered my efforts. I was wondering, will history repeat itself?

At least this time I was wearing an all polypropylene and Gore-Tex jacket. I was still cold though and wondered why. Being 25 years older than during my earlier climb, and perhaps not in top shape and quite weary, may have accounted for it. The cold forced me to turn west, reach the upper south slopes of Mt. McHarg and put my bivouac there. It took a bit of will power to expose a few frames of the Royal Group by moonlight. Then I called it a day. It was not too comfortable but later on the wind abated and allowed me to sleep well.

This time I did not resort to my bottle of brandy. Morning

greeted me with typical autumn weather – crisp, calm and cold. I was in perfect position and quickly took a few shots of the Royal Group, bronzed by the rising sun, with monumental Mt. King George (3422m) standing silently across Palliser River to the west. Then without delay, feasting on a delicious wild berry power bar, I headed for the summit 45 minutes away.

Easy to access, the summit greeted me with a 'WOW' views, especially to the north, where gray, ugly looking Mt. Sir Douglas (3406m) looked very impressive, but ominous. Had I reached the summit the previous day, I would have photographed this giant dressed up in the reddish hues of sunrise. To the northwest, Mt. Assiniboine graced the horizon. East of Mt. Sir Douglas, Mt. Robertson, French and Jellicoe presented their million-year old southern faces. The south horizon is dominated by Mt. Joffre (3450m). Three Isle Lake was a great disappointment though – by late autumn this usually pretty lake had receded so much, it looked like a half dried up slough. To make it worse, I could not see the entire lake from the true summit because the northeast ridge obscured it. The day turned out to be gorgeous, calm and sunny so I took my photos, had a small

breakfast, dried my 'stuff' and it was time to leave this pleasant hospitable summit. On the way back, I discovered a shorter way to the lake. I also discovered below the Col in the meadows numerous fresh diggings for ground squirrels. A Grizzly was somewhere nearby. I did not ask question, kept my pepper spray handy, and ran down the slope as fast as I could. I had an contingency plan in case that Grizzly tried to charge - I would simply take away his credit cards!

I have seen many Bear diggings in the past. Some squirrels dig their nests one meter or deeper. Some dig under big boulders or large tree roots. On a high open meadow, they dig deeper, maybe 1.5m, but this is no big deal for a Bear. I have seen huge craters dug by a hungry Bear, at the bottom an empty nest. It always makes me wonder whether a squirrel really understands the dangers of living in Bear country! On the other hand, where is the 'economical sense' on the Bear's part to dig nearly two meters, expending so much energy, for a tiny squirrel snack?

Most mountains have their own unique characteristics. For example, Mt. Worthington has rocks so sharp and rough that any contact means scratches and cuts. You cannot sit on them and your boots wear out very quickly. On the way down by Mt. Indefatigable trail, a sign read: 'Aggressive Grizzly in the area, trail closed.' I was glad my van was just a few minutes away.

Another story from long ago was when I climbed Ptarmigan Peak (3059m) located northeast of Lake Louise, along the trail to Deception Pass. A nice, easy scramble but the weather was hazy and humid in early summer, so I could not get any decent photos. Later on I went in late September and this time it looked all right. Just as I approached the vegetation limit, a small Goat's half-eaten body caught my eye – a potentially dangerous situation. It was a certainty that a Cougar was near guarding its meal until the last bone was consumed. It is unwise to hang around a kill because if there are two Cougars, they could easily make a sumptuous meal of you. So I departed immediately, looking back frequently. The scramble was quite long but easy. I reached the summit early enough to look around, leisurely set up my shelter and get ready for 'shootout' at sunset. Conditions were not bad - a bit hazy - producing rather poor light. The evening turned out to be pleasant with a large moon casting enough light to photograph by.

I set up the camera to the north and worked on Polaris, then shooting east over Deception Pass towards the two giants, Mt. Douglas and Mt. St. Bride. Next morning the rising sun burst on the scene with strong light for about 15 seconds; suddenly a large cloud on the eastern sky obscured the sunlight. I watched with disappointment and disbelief - that cloud would not move an inch for the next two hours. The main purpose of the trip was to photograph the two Skoki Lakes to the north in early morning light. The whole valley to the north was all dressed up with golden Larch trees, further up were endless mountains and blue sky, like a beautiful dream. I figured if I could get other photos, it would be like an extra bonus for my efforts. I had plenty of time for breakfast, packed my gear and relaxed. I was resigned to the fact I would never get a photo of those lakes.

Around 10 a.m. I noticed a slow movement of those ugly, stubborn and inconsiderate clouds. Big deal, I thought! I spent the night here to take photos in low morning light and, finally, I might get something at noon, which I consider the worst light for photography. Suddenly out of the blue, or rather gray, the sun started burning off those clouds so rapidly that within a few minutes there was bright sunshine all over the place. Without delay, I shot a number of frames using different lenses and voila! Thanks a lot, mission accomplished! The pictures were quite acceptable and a few of them are featured in this volume. Ascending I had taken the southeast route and descended via a prominent gully straight south; hence, I never discovered what progress the Cougar made on that poor little Goat.

This area has always been my favourite playground; I have climbed several peaks here: Fossil Mountain and Mt. Richardson, three times; Oyster Peak, Skoki Mountain, and Heather Ridge. I visited the area four times in the winter – a lovely part of the Rockies.

My winter attempt to climb Mt. Richardson (3086m) located 10 km northeast of Lake Louise, was indeed memorable. It was late winter, but in the Rockies, April is still considered winter, period. I set out early in the morning and all went very smooth and uneventful. By the time I reached the open area around Half Way Hut, I noticed the snow was getting soft - I soon broke through and fell down two or three times. As I reached Hidden Lake at higher elevation, the snow became harder. From here I scrambled west, to a very steep slope, in order to access South Ridge.

The day was wonderfully sunny, temperature comfortable, but a bit windy. After hard slogging, I reached the ridge, exposed to open spaces, with the westerly wind gusting to probably 100 km/h. In the blink of an eye, I was pushed east towards that steep slope. Miraculously, I lay down flat and anchored myself with my ski poles in the snow. Instinctively I decided to get out of that wind below the ridge. It was around noon, a gorgeous clear day, before I got over the initial shock and tried to assess my situation. I tried testing the wind by going closer to the ridge, but found it to be even stronger. Since I had enough time to spare, I had a small snack, for a while admiring the scenery, and rested.

Half an hour later, I checked the wind again; it was as strong as before. The temperature on that windy ridge was very uncomfortable. The entire summit was enveloped in huge white flurries and a blizzard. I realized I was defeated by the elements and it would be too risky to continue. It was the first time ever that I was forced to quit before reaching the summit. Feeling defeated, I descended that steep slope and soon reached Hidden Lake. In the sheltered valley, the afternoon temperature rose considerably rendering the snow too soft to continue. I broke through the snow and fell down a four foot hole – it took a while to get out only to fall in again a few feet further on. The snow just kept collapsing under my weight. The sun was frying that snow mercilessly and the farther I descended, the softer the snow became. It was not my day! I began to realize I was in quite a predicament. I had visions of having to remain there for two months until all that snow melted. But, there's always a solution to every problem. So I turned around and headed north towards Boulder Pass, reasoning that temperatures higher up in the open would be lower and the snow harder. And it was! After exploring the area around Ptarmigan Lake, I retired for the night. I slept very soundly as the temperature dropped to -10°C. I had a plan and it worked. I rose early and skied down as fast as I could on that firmly frozen snow. I reached the highway before the strong spring sun could soften the snow again. A hard lesson learned, but soon forgotten, since I got into the very same predicament by Mt. Assiniboine a few years later. Mountaineering may look simple and great fun, but it is not always so.

Any problems encountered 20km deep in the wilderness can not only be serious, but also tragic. Be prepared. It is wise to take food for one or two days more than your intended stay; also extra warm clothes are essential. Let someone reliable know where you are going and register your trip with the proper authority. If you fail to return at the appointed time, rescue efforts will be launched the next day. You will be found and helped if you are in trouble – this is a free service. Should you, however, fail to return for some frivolous reason, necessitating rescue efforts, you most certainly could be charged the costs incurred by the rescue team. So play it safe and smart.

MOUNTAIN WISE

How to get to the mountain, enjoy the trip, and live to tell the story? For young people, everything is great, cool, and no problem, even when there are a lot of problems. Somehow when they fall, they invariably land on all 'four feet'. The older you get, the more you realize how dangerous and unforgiving mountains can be. Numbers speak volumes – it is estimated nearly a thousand people get killed worldwide, in an average year while mountaineering, and five time more are injured. Novices get hurt the most, but even very experienced climbers die, not necessarily due to mistakes, but natural hazards like avalanches, slides, lightning, etc. Many injuries occur when crossing creeks or rivers; rocks and logs can be quite deadly when wet and slippery. The wilderness and mountains present various hazards and real danger, so before heading into the wild, you should become familiar with possible problems. Learn as much as possible about the areas you plan to visit.

Carry detailed maps and a compass, especially when visiting flat, wooded wilderness. When hiking, look for easy-to-remember landmarks so you can find your way back. Pay special attention at junctions of two or more trails; taking a wrong turn means ending up in the wrong place. When camping overnight, even if you get lost, you will survive the night. If you get lost on a day trip without survival gear, you may find yourself in rather a dicey situation. Some people carry basic survival equipment, even on a day trip, such as, a foam pad, bivouac or plastic tube as rain protection, a light summer sleeping bag, maybe a blanket, plus an extra sweater and food. The weight is not too much and it can definitely save your life, especially in late autumn or winter. If you break a leg or get hopelessly lost and night is approaching, make yourself a nest of dried vegetation, or mosses, and cover yourself with a thick layer of evergreen branches. You will survive the night.

For a camping trip of two or more days duration, you must be prepared for weather changes, from hot to cold, and dry to wet. Take enough clothes to cope with all circumstances. Rain gear, warm clothing, sturdy boots, spare socks, gloves, hat, sunglasses, and sunscreen, are 'musts'. In cold seasons, plan on layered clothing. Start from the skin out: if your underwear is cotton, and gets wet, your body will lose heat 25 times faster than if you wore a dry garment. Use polyester or polypropylene for the inner layer. In cold weather, use two layers; it will transpose your body's moisture to the next layer, evaporate, keeping you dry and warm. Wool dries slowly and is very heavy when wet. Use synthetic middle layers, like pile or fleece, which are light weight, durable, warm and inexpensive. When the weather is windy and wet, wear a breathable and waterproof Gore-Tex jacket. On cold days, protect your head, hands and feet, not to mention your torso. The fact is, that 50% of body heat loss happens through the head and neck being unprotected. Proper wear protects the body from heat loss, because as you hike, ski or climb, you lose energy (heat). This loss must be replaced quickly or you will be in danger of developing hypothermia.

When mountaineering, do not indulge in decadent or extravagant menus, unless you want to hire two Sherpas to carry your entire kitchen. All you need is zesty, simple foods, which contain carbohydrates, fat and protein. Items containing sugar are essential as they are rapidly converted into energy.

Power bars, chocolate, honey biscuits, nuts or dried fruits, are excellent energy producers. On longer trips, vitamins and minerals are also beneficial. Snacking often produces consistent energy and does not overload your system like a large meal does. Some suggestions for dinner are: fresh lobster, filet mignon or lasagna, carried in a cooler? Or, just settle for a freeze-dried complete meal in a pouch, which requires adding hot water and presto, dinner's ready! It is light, odorless until opened, and the shelf life is practically unlimited. Downside: the price is high. There are dry foods only slightly heavier and are much cheaper. Bulk foods are still cheaper. Pasta or noodle dishes, with cheese, and some spices make fine meals. Oats, granola with milk, hot chocolate, nuts, sugar and dried fruit, make for an adequate delicious and zesty breakfast.

Nuts are hard to crack, especially almonds. Soak them in water for 24 hours, or better yet, in wine or brandy, before use and you won't break a tooth. One or two apples a day are also good for you. On hot days, you need to drink at least three litres of water; in winter, even more to prevent dehydration, which can be very hazardous to your health. Dehydration can weaken your mental sharpness and physical ability to perform, which may cause serious accidents and even death. To carry water for several days is impossible, so you will need to rely on water being available wherever you are going. Boiling water for 10-15 minutes is the most reliable method of purification; using chemicals or filtration is your second choice, and not as reliable as boiling. Untreated water may contain nasty parasites, which can get you into major or long-term difficulties.

Camping in the wilderness is potentially troublesome. We have the attitude that if we pay a camping fee, we have some rights or special privileges. The wilderness, however, is home to a lot of wild critters, whose territory we are invading. Unfortunately, these toothy residents do not recognize our camping permits. From a wee Mouse to a nasty Packrat to a Weasel, Wolverine or even a Bear, they are all either curious to know who we are, or they simply want to sample our strange smelling foods. Some precautions, which may keep our vittles safe from these nosy wilderness denizens, are as follows: Cook all meals 100 meters downwind from your camp. Keep your kitchen meticulously clean. Hang aromatic foods in a heavy duty sack on a 'bear pole' at the campsite, or on a line suspended between two trees, at least four meters above the ground. Of course, some rodents and birds will still be able to get at your food dangling on the line. Some campsites now have food storage facilities, which are one hundred percent animal-proof.

No one has yet come up with a foolproof solution to handling hungry and unpredictable Bears. A Bear is not a man eater who will ambush or attack from behind. Bears kill other animals, or will eat carrion, but basically they will stay away from humans, except when surprised. Bears have no natural predators, thus they have no fear. All animals stay clear, well away from the Bear. So if you find yourself face to face with a Bear, surprise one, the Bear may view this as an attack, and will usually take defensive action, with predictable outcome. When you are walking on the trail and are approaching a blind bend ahead, make noise and clatter to warn the Bear of your presence. Since most animals are voiceless, sharp, loud noises irritate and frighten them. Group

hiking provides the best security – it is almost unheard of for a Bear to attack ten people.

Bear spray? Some say, it provides a false sense of security, but is really of little use. Can you stop a locomotive in ten meters? When a 400 kg Bear charges at you at 40km/h, it won't be stopped on the spot because of a little spray. The Bear may knock you down, inflict some injury, then run away, or it may just sit down for a few minutes sobbing and suffering the effects of the spray. One trend of thought is to spray the Bear again, then run as fast as you can. Still another solution that may be effective is to climb a tree if you can do it fast enough. A Bear can reach to nearly four meters and some Grizzlies can climb a bit as well.

Another unpleasant critter to be on the lookout for is the Cougar. People very seldom see this big cat, which does not mean that only few are in existence. Cougars are quite common throughout the Rockies and are formidable hunters. The Cougar will sit in the bush alongside a game trail and wait. When the right-sized prey happens along, the Cougar attacks from behind. A lone child, small person, Deer or Goat, are fair game and could become a meal for a hungry Cougar. In British Columbia's wilderness, children, house pets and domestic animals, are attacked every year by this ferocious big cat.

It is important to know who is who and where, but millions of happy campers enjoy the wilderness without ever being bothered by wild animals. Again, if you go with a group of four or more, stay together, do not split or separate. Your wilderness experience will be nothing short of pure joy and very memorable good clean fun.

One important mountain feature should not be overlooked – the avalanche. According to the law of gravity, what goes up must come down. Rock slides, or even a single falling rock, can kill you if you are in its path. But the really ferocious, silent killer, is the unpredictable snow and ice avalanche. It sneaks up so quickly and quietly that by the time you notice the monster bearing down on you, it is often too late to take any evasive action. Avalanches can be 20 meters or one kilometer in width. Sliding, tumbling down through a narrow gully, or an entire slope can come down, crushing everything in its path, including mature dense forests, mountain huts, and cabins. Entire villages have been swept away in the Alps and the Himalayas, where human population is dense. How does one recognize avalanche terrain and its timing? Primarily, leeward slopes are more avalanche-prone than windward slopes. The latter have wind-packed snow, thus they are more stable. Leeward slopes receive blown and drifted snow which creates unstable slabs. In the Rockies, dangerous leeward slopes are usually on the east and southeast. Slopes of 30°-50° steepness, with smooth configurations, are more avalanche-prone than those with rugged, steep or flatter surfaces.

Long periods of clear weather can create a frosty crust on the packed snow surface. Then along comes a heavy 50cm snowfall. The new dry snow cannot bond with its icy base – a sure recipe for a disaster, an avalanche is almost imminent. A large party of skiers on such a slope, combined with strong winds, can trigger a slide. The avalanche is a merciless white killer. To avoid a tragedy, you must know the nature of the beast. Anyone venturing into the mountains in winter should become familiar with avalanches by reading some well documented books. An absolute necessity is to carry an avalanche rescue beacon, a shovel and probe, and never, ever go alone.

A very useful hint if you find yourself trapped by avalanche snow: if you are conscious and breathing, you may be covered by as little as 50cm of snow, but you do not know which direction to dig to safety. Try to clear some space in front of you, then make a snowball and release it. Dig fast in the direction opposite to where the ball fell – you have only 10-15 minutes of oxygen supply before your time is up. You may have seen skiers sitting on an avalanche path, having a snack or just enjoying the view. It is really a good place to get killed. You must cross an avalanche patch or shut as fast as you can and keep looking up the slope. Safety in the wintry mountains depends to a large degree on your wisdom, knowledge and ability. Get to know the snow and you should be able to outsmart and outlive an avalanche.

PHOTOGRAPHY

A professional studio photographer once asked me, how long it took to shoot photos for a book on the Rockies. Two to three years was my answer. Very surprised, he proclaimed, it would take him three to four months. That's a typical re action; not many people understand or appreciate what is involved in photographing mountains. Even if you photograph the Rockies from the shoulder of the road, or from a helicopter, you still have to contend with weather conditions. You are dealing with nearly 1000km long stretch of mountains. It is safe to say that in an entire year, there may only be 30-40 days that are perfect for professional photography. For over half the summer, the air is humid and wet, and not conducive for photographing. Forest fires, autumn slush burning by loggers, can ruin photography for months. The winter's cold does not allow adequate searching for photography either. Actually August and September are the best months to get decent shooting done. So-called accidental photos do happen occasionally, completely unplanned, and unexpected. Driving along in heavy rain, and suddenly a huge double rainbow comes into view, or the Aurora Borealis suddenly adorns the sky, or a Grizzly or Wolf crosses the road directly in front of your car. These situations require having your camera at the ready, fast action and a lot of luck.

Some pro photographers shoot only at first light or low light, and penetrate deep into the mountains. Others may shoot at noon from a car window – both claim to be photographers. Those who can afford it, use helicopters, and they too think of themselves as mountain photographers. Say or think what you will, there is really only one way to do honest professional mountain photography, and that is, to pack up and go deep into the mountains for several day at a time. Hike, climb, bivouac on the mountain, rain or shine, you are in the middle of the action, and action you will get.

You may witness roaring avalanches, blinding blizzards, downpours of rain, peaceful flowery meadows, lush green valleys, purple red sunset glow, or a black sky canopy richly studded with twinkling silvery stars. You must know and understand the subject to be photographed. It, of course, helps if you passionately love it as well.

Some back country trips net five to ten quality photos, some net zero, due to less than ideal conditions. You lick your wounds, recover, and go again and again. You may make 15 trips a year, and if luck is with you, you may produce 40-50 quality photos.

Another example of what's in store for a pro outdoors photographer: a picturesque lake is nestled alongside the road, easy to access by car. You come before sunrise, set up your camera and wait. The sky is clear, the water calm, all is perfect for a great shot. You wait and wait and the sun does not rise! On the eastern horizon, a small band of clouds have obscured the sun. Ten minutes later, the sun bursts with bright light on the lake, but the reddish colour, which lasts for about 30-60 seconds when the sun emerges on the horizon, is gone, no colour. Not one to give up, you come next morning and all is perfect, but the wind creates choppy water, no reflections. Next try, the sky is totally overcast. Undaunted, the following morning all is superb. Full of hope, you set up the camera, the sunlight is just touching the top of the mountains with gorgeous reddish hues and…..a few curious ducks decide to come and investigate what you are up to. All of a sudden that beautiful mirror-like lake surface, the reflections, are gone. Lucky for those ducks, they do not realize what that poor photographer thinks of them!! Oh, yes, you come again, and all was not bad, except the air was hazy and brownish, and no great photo will be taken. So you see, one may visit that lake ten or fifteen times and not produce one high quality image. Question: How much does it cost for all these trips? When you finally capture that great shot, publishers try to purchase it for $25, including all rights.

Are you tired of reading all that bad news? Well here's just one more: Waterton's Buffalo Paddock offers grand possibilities for a fine shot: the great furry beasts with the Rockies as background. You arrive in the morning, light condition are right, but where are the Buffalo? They are hiding somewhere behind one of the dozens of small hills. You can't see them as they may sojourn there for an hour or longer. Not to be discouraged, you return again in the late afternoon and now the Buffalo are a long distance from the road, over by a very 'photogenic high fence'. You wait, but the Buffalo today are moving at a snail's pace, so again, no deal! Next day, it rains cats and dogs. The time after that, the Buffalo are taking a one-hour break on the far side of a slough, just resting and peacefully chewing their cud. So while some photographers try ten times and don't get one decent shot, other folks drive in for the first time and the 'Buffs' are behaving admirably, smiling and posing for perfect photos.

A pro nature photographer met a tourist from Europe, first time in Canada, who encountered two Wolves and shot several frames of quality photos at very close range. Other people who have lived here for years and shoot for a living, maybe see a Wolf once, at a distance. Outdoor photography requires time and patience – plenty of both. If you lack these attributes, forget it, photograph fried chicken commercials or weddings.

These frustrations along the road are no big deal – they are included here to inject some gray humour. The committed outdoors photographer drives home, enjoys a nice repast, and life goes on.

Picture this scenario of what a real mountain photographer faces. The forecast calls for sunny weather for the next three days. So he sets out, walks for 15km, then climbs up a 3000m mountain. It is nearing sundown as he approaches the summit and he notices rather ominous looking clouds approaching. He builds a shelter hurriedly and crawls in. The wind is howling like a hungry Wolf and the shelter is on the verge of getting blown away. Next comes the driving rain, temperature plummets below freezing and it begins snowing heavily. Needless to say, the thought crosses his mind – will he survive the night and get down off that steep snowy mountain next day? Then again, the inclement weather may continue for two or three days, or maybe only a few hours. He remembers the forecast - three sunny days. Well, c'est la vie! He cannot blame the weatherman. Predicting weather accurately in the mountains is almost impossible. So if you go for a hike on a sunny day, take rain gear; when it rains, take sunscreen. If you feel warm and have enough supplies, you may remain on that snowy peak one more night, waiting for favourable photographing conditions.

If the weather continues hostile, try to get down as quickly as possible. At 300m below the summit, there will be no snow. It will be much warmer and less windy. So, you spent two days in the deep freeze, walked 30km, with no photos to write home about; at least you managed to collect a few nasty blisters.

Many people claim that one out of three or four trips like the above are really a success photo-wise. You may ask, why do people do it, where is the fun in it? Fun? It is beyond fun, it is an adventure like no other, an endurance test, and the satisfaction of proving that you can do it. When you survive an ordeal such as this, you feel victorious over the elements: blizzards, cold, wind, all very threatening, but you have survived it and lived to tell the story.

This may sound like a teen's talk of bravado – we all know that people sometimes get hurt and even killed in the unforgiving world of mountaineering. To be young and talk brave may be expected and somewhat normal, but when a mature man challenges high mountains solo, some say, he should either have his head examined or be awarded the Order of Canada for bravery! Mountaineering gets in your blood, it becomes a habit, very addictive. You cannot stop, you just keep at it as long as you can walk. Some mountaineers say: 'I would rather get killed up there than be run over by a drunk driver on a city street.'

Mountaineering, when done sensibly, is a tremendously healthy and challenging sport, and can be relatively safe. Combine the physical prowess it takes to conquer a mountain with artistic eyes to see nature's beauty, and you have created a full-fledged mountain photographer. This is a breed that is not very plentiful.

What equipment, cameras, does a mountain photographer use? Most photographers work with a 35mm single reflex camera, primarily because of its small size and light weight. Still others carry medium format, but almost no one carries a large format to the top of a mountain, unless he can afford a Sherpa to carry it. For backpacking and longer trekking, you might take two cameras, lenses: 20,28,50,100,200mm, or as required, a small tripod, a good variety of film; oh, and don't forget spare batteries. Pack all of it in heavy plastic bag(s) for protection from the elements. When travelling in below freezing temperatures, keep cameras under your parka and inside your sleeping bag at night. You rise before the sun does, determine what you want to shoot, and from where; it may require walking up or down for some distance. Make sure you eat a snack or two to elevate blood sugar levels to boost your energy. If you are not fully alert, you may fall or get injured. A large piece of chocolate, or a power bar, washed down with water will do the trick nicely. It will also enhance your creativity and zest for life, so essential to great photography.

Be on the lookout for Bears, which often visit campgrounds looking for food scraps. A surprised Bear will construe your presence as a threat and will act in self-defense. The outcome is predictable – you probably won't be taking photos any more. Make your presence known – create noise.

How to photograph wildlife? Short answer: Very carefully. All animals are wild and could be potentially dangerous, even if they appear tame. They have you figured out better than you do them. To them, you are slow, clumsy and weak, as compared to most large animals. Moose, Elk, and even Deer, can inflict serious injury or even death. A Bear is not to be fooled with under any circumstances. 400 kg bulk of muscle may kill a man with one sweep. Never, ever approach a Bear closer than 80 or 100 meters. Black Bears have a somewhat milder temper than the Grizzly, but both will kill a few people each year. They should be treated with due respect and realistic fear. Unless you are in the company of a large group, if you see a Grizzly, leave the area fast. Pepper spray may give a false sense of security but it is really not much help. The best answer to a Bear problem is to travel in groups and make lots of noise. You must have read about this Grizzly incident: When killed by Grizzly, photographer's film was processed. The last photo appeared to be taken from ten meters. So much for silliness!

Female wild animals are very protective of their young and can be extremely dangerous. They should not be approached at distances closer than 60-70 meters. A mama and two cute babies are always very tempting for any cameraman, but it may cost you. Moose have been known to charge, knock one down, and trample one to a pulp. Watch the Moose's eyes – if she looks upset and its ears are down, exit without delay. It is best to approach game very slowly, bend down so as not to loom large and threatening. Do not stare at the animal, move very gently, speaking softly. Stop for a while, then move a bit closer. The animal will realize your non-threatening behaviour and get used to your presence. In this way, you can get up very close to photograph a relaxed, natural animal. Of course, all of the latter does not apply to Grizzly Bear.

Cougars are very plentiful all over the mountains. You may not see them, but they see you. The Cougar, a hunter, follows people, but in such a clever way that you are not aware of it. At first snow, go up and return the same way, and you may see Cougar tracks right in your footprints. It may sound scary but it is real. A small person alone could become a Cougar feast. If a Cougar can kill a Deer, Elk, or even a Moose, what chance would you have? Take the illusive, invisible big cat very seriously, especially in winter, look back once in a while. All those 'pussy cats" you see in publications are photographed at game parks and are domestically raised. To shoot a quality photo of a wild Cougar is almost impossible; the same goes for Wolf, but to a lesser extent.

Photographing small animals, rodents and birds, requires much more effort, patience and special equipment. Motor drive and 300-600mm lens is a must. Photographing wildlife is exciting and dangerous, but very rewarding. There is nothing like expecting the unexpected. The surprise factor. Surprising a Grizzly may end badly, yet we are willing to take that risk with little hesitation.

It is worth mentioning that 'close-up' is a very creative and rewarding form of photography. A simple shot of a flower, plant, insect, a berry or fallen leaf, is pretty and easy to get. All you need is a 50 or 100mm macro lens, point, shoot, and voila! For extreme macro work, fancy equipment and more know how is required.

With the advent of digital cameras, colour manipulating and enhancing have become the way for many. Graduated filters and more tricks are coming every day. It is difficult to produce pure, natural photography. However, many serious photo journalists, especially self-respecting nature photographers, would never touch these phony gadgets. They would rather use old cameras which allow them to produce what they intend. Nature photography is great fun, whether professional or recreational, because it brings out the best in a person, and develops a gentle and sensitive character with a keen appreciation of beauty. Keep photographing, break a tripod!

NOCTURNAL PHOTOGRAPHY

It is hard to determine the popularity of night photography, but it is a fact that people are constantly fascinated with these mysterious illusive nocturnal images. Not many people shoot at night for many and varied reasons. A day shot takes, say, 1/100 of a second while a night photo may require ° or a one hour time factor. Extra equipment is needed, as well as a heavy tripod. You must be away from car or city lights with no wind, basically calm. Often you set up night shooting near the road, start exposing (it may be midnight or later) and out of the blue or rather black, a policeman or park warden patrol car will show up, , bright lights flashing, red emergency flashers on, and the concerned officer asks: "Having problems?" or "What are you doing here after midnight?" You are tempted to politely (sic) tell him: "Yes, officer, the problem is you.' Of course, you respond: "I am taking photos, sir", whereupon he responds: "Taking photos, you say, taking photos in the dark? Your driving license please." Only after you show him the camera sitting on the tripod does the officer relax somewhat, but often by then it is too late for you, the glaring lights ruin the photo.

You rewind and start on the next frame, hoping all the officers are safely back home snoring the night away. A strong wind may shake your camera and ruin everything, but the night photographer's worst enemy is moisture. With the absence of the sun, there may be moisture in the air, even when the sky is completely clear. If that moisture settles on your lens, the photos will be fuzzy and virtually useless .

The problem is you cannot use a flashlight to check your lens for wetness, so you gamble and maybe waste an hour. A helpful hint: you can touch the metal tripod and if it is wet, you may be sure the lens is as well wet. You can also take lens tissue and wipe the moisture off every 15 minutes, trying not to shake your camera in the process. When photographing in below freezing temperature, make sure to set up your tripod and let it sit for five minutes. The tripod will melt into the ground and freeze there; then you start your exposure.

If you are working on top of the mountain, it is a differ-ent ballgame. A mountain shutterbug's life is…mostly cold, and the life span of his camera is short. Wind is a bitter enemy and at the heights it is seldom comfortably warm, so the photographer and camera both suffer. It is not an unusual scenario, even in summer: after huddling in your shelter for an hour of night time exposure, you bring your camera inside and notice the lens is still open, frozen. Just put a lens cap on, slip the camera into your sleeping bag, and wait for the 'click' when the camera thaws – this may take five or ten minutes. If you are so inclined, you may try another exposure, if not, just wrap yourself up tight and try to get some shut-eye.

What do you catch on film after one hour night exposure? Star treks – curving lines of different thickness and colour. Most certainly the film will capture shooting stars, meteorites, satellites, jet liners leaving solid or dashed colourful tracks. If you are shooting due north, chances are you will capture the Northern Lights or traces of same. Or you may see a bright colourful glow along the horizon, which seems to be present most nights, especially in late autumn and winter.

Here is what might happen to a night photographer in extreme conditions: You bivouac on the top of a 3200m ice and snow-covered mountain, where it is bitter cold and the sky is clear. Having no tripod, you make a stand by piling snow, set your camera for long exposure, and retreat to your sleeping bag to survive. Your day was long and rough, the big climb expended a lot of energy. Tiredness set in and you went to sleep. Near morning, you awaken and recall there is something to be done. Not being sure what it might be, you turn over and go back to sleep. Morning comes, and you are facing a new challenge, a heavy snowfall overnight has dumped a foot of white fluff. Goodness gracious, you realize that your camera is out there…but where? Everything is white and flat! After searching, you bump into that little 'tripod' and retrieve a completely snow-covered and frozen solid camera.

Descending from that snowy slippery mountain proves to be challenging and dangerous. But, what about the night photo? Oh well, it turned out 'slightly' over-exposed, about eight hours or so! There are those who insist that night photography is easy. You set your camera on a tripod, nap in your car for an hour or two, and when you awake, the camera may be gone. To be on the safe side, place the camera in bush cover and try not to sleep: Instead, watch that marvelous night sky and visually enjoy what your camera is seeing, a great celestial show is constantly unfolding, one which you won't soon forget. Was Beethoven watching the night sky before composing 'Moonlight Sonata', one wonder? More than likely.

Shooting the Northern Lights is more challenging than it may appear to be. It is seldom that quality photos of this awesome phenomenon can be captured from this far south. You need to travel into the vicinity of the 60th parallel to capture this magnificent extravaganza. Aurora ('dawn' in Latin) Borealis arouses such passion in serious photographers that they will travel north, spend many dollars, and suffer winter discomfort, to get quality photos. A heavy tripod, fast film, fast lens, fast mind and hands, help to capture this unique natural wonder.

You need time and unlimited patience to circumvent adverse conditions because the Aurora does not occur every night. For this reason, capturing one is so precious and exciting. When and where? October to March when nights are long, anywhere in the world, but close to circumpolar regions offers the best chances. In the Southern Hemisphere, exactly the same phenomenon occurs, known as 'Aurora Australis'.

WATERTON TALK

In October when trees and shrubs turn into a rich palette of colour, and the air is crisp and cool, it is time to visit the southern Rockies: Waterton Lakes National Park, in particular. Animals start their annual migration from high meadows and valleys into low flats east of Waterton Village. It is not unusual to spot herds of 100 or more Elk. Deer, Moose and Sheep gather here as well, always followed by predators, such as the Wolf, Coyote and Cougar, looking for a meal.

Grizzly and Black Bears feed frantically on abundant berries and other edible matter to gain enough fat to sustain them through the ordeal of over five months of winter hibernation. Crowsnest Pass' (1357m) low elevation allows warm Pacific air to flow into the Prairies year round, which, in winter, is a blessing in many ways. A strong westerly wind, called 'Chinook' melts or blows away the snow, allowing grazing animals easy access to their food source. Temperatures fluctuate with wind intensity and can reach well above freezing in January. When the wind subsides and a major Arctic weather system pushes south, within a matter of hours, the mercury may drop to -30°C. It can remain there for several days, dumping plenty of snow, until the next powerful Chinook pushes it east. These days can be very hard on many animals wintering here, causing some to die.

The southern Rockies are undoubtedly very attractive landscape-wise, and wildlife is the most plentiful here of all the Rockies. Summer and autumn are ideal but spring can hold many surprises. Rolling hills, which are moraines created by the last ice age glacier, are comprised of gravel, clay and sedimentary silt. They appear to be bone dry, barely supporting little grasses here and there, yet…in May, the northerly shaded slopes of these moraines are loaded with gorgeous bright yellow glacier lilies and purple prairie crocuses – a spectacular sight to behold. Worth mentioning is another unique spectacle of Waterton Park the showy Bear Grass, which can be seen in mid-summer at its northern limit of growth.

You may wonder why Waterton Park is so small, and yet ecologically, the valuable area north of the Park is not protected. Why not enlarge the Park in Alberta and British Columbia north to Crowsnest Pass? Most of the land there belongs to the Crown, so it should not be a costly proposition. The east and west 'enlarged' Park's boundary could feature a low speed scenic highway, with tourist services located outside of the Park to maintain National Park standards. With the extra space, the existing Buffalo Paddock could be enlarged to a length of ten kilometers and could accommodate, not 20, but 200 of these fascinating hardy creatures. This enhanced Waterton Park would undoubtedly become the most attractive National Park in Canada

for viewing wild game, not to mention protecting a large tract of wilderness from inevitable development. Let's go for it now, before the bulldozers get there!

Canada, being such a large country, could well afford larger National Parks. For example, Wood Buffalo National Park is greater in area than Switzerland, but it is located in the far northern 'wasteland' where the hostile climate limits human presence. Fauna, as well, face inhospitable conditions and, therefore, three or four times more land is needed to sustain animals as in the south.

The southern Rockies, and the Prairies to the east, are notorious for severe drought, sometimes for several consecutive years. By August most of the small creeks (run-off from snowy slopes) are completely dry. By September, large creeks and even rivers, are almost dry. The arid, warm Chinooks, dry everything to the bone. One advantage of these winds is the wind-generated electric power. More turbines are being installed each year east of Crowsnest Pass so, hopefully, soon all of southern Alberta will be using this clean source of electricity. Nowadays, it seems that man can alter anything, even climate. We cannot stop the land eroding Chinook, but in order to bring more moisture to the region, more water is needed. How? One way is to build power generating dams on the larger creeks and rivers, for instance, twenty on both sides of the Great Divide. Evaporation creates moist microclimate, clouds and rain. Moose and Beaver would be delighted and Prairie agriculture would benefit as well.

Now the driest Park, Waterton, with all these new lakes could be a fishing paradise and a limited water sports park, with no power boats allowed, only canoes, on the lower 25% of the lake. The upper 75% of the lake could be reserved for Moose, nesting waterfowl, fish and frogs, which would make the Otter happy as well.

A growing population causes the wilderness to shrink and eventually disappear. Once large development occurs, it cannot be contained or removed, it will only grow. So let's pretend, we have enlarged Waterton to Crowsnest Pass – now we ought to connect it with Banff National Park to the north. In that way, the entire backbone of the Rockies would be protected, from the 49th parallel to Kakwa Park north of Mt. Robson. Further north, where human presence is very scarce, there is not much concern about the wilderness. Mining, oil exploration, logging and hunting, are strictly regulated and controlled by government and the harsh northern climate will take care of the environment.

It is imperative that a safe continuous corridor is maintained for wildlife to move south or north freely. When mining north of Crowsnest Pass is over, we must make sure mining companies restore land to its natural state. No development should be allowed within 30km east and west of the Great Divide, the site of future Tornado National Park. Knowing how governments work, one can only say: "Yeah, good luck, keep on dreaming." In our society, generally when many people want government to do something, government will comply. So let's demand that the government enlarges Waterton Park and creates new Tornado National Park to the north. In this way, the entire length of the majestic Rockies wilderness would be protected. Write to Ottawa today!

HEALTH AND ENVIRONMENT

Health and environment are closely related and depend on each other. The term 'environment' is derived from the French: environner – environ and virer – around, and define the surrounding area or outskirts of a particular site. Today environmental issues reflect our concerns about the environment or the condition of our surroundings. In a broader sense, we also refer or think of the environment as wilderness, natural green areas being invaded, overtaken by fast-growing urban developments, and eventually destroyed. Since more than half the population reside in cities, it is critical that we take better care of our urban environment. Where not long ago stood endless woods, great pristine wilderness, full of life wetlands, today we see large city sprawls, where millions of people exist in questionable living conditions, which can hardly be called 'healthy'.

We are talking here about 'humungous' conglomerates of over three million people, where trees cannot survive and die, just as humans do. Toxic fumes from millions of cars, factories, heating systems, create a thick umbrella of pollution over cities. Their inhabitants are left with little choice but to inhale poisoned air, day by day, until they sicken and die prematurely.

A visionary, concerned urbanist, who knows and cares will ask: Why don't we plan and build our cities so living conditions in them would be just that – 'living' , not just existing? Why not indeed? After all, our health, life and environment are closely connected. Yes, it would be possible to build a healthy city environment. The ideal city with a humane face would be no more than one million population, measure no more than 250 square kilometers, and have at least 25 one square kilometer of parks, lakes and densely tree-lined streets. More people would live in high-rise apartments and condo towers, less in single family dwellings, which accounts for the dreaded urban sprawl.

All office buildings would be 30 stories or higher, to keep the area of the city small. Small, because when a city reaches a certain size, a freeze would go into effect and no more growth would be allowed. Just for the sake of conjecture, to illustrate how to fight the horror of urban sprawl, imagine this, not exactly Utopian, but realistic concept. All city buildings are 50 stories tall, 400 of them would accommodate one million people on less than 100 square kilometres. Are we talking land use economy here? Almost walking distance to work, no cars needed, small, less expensive infrastructure, would allow for low taxes. Pollution would not accumulate and linger, there would be no more two-hour commutes to work, etc. And just picture the view from the swimming pools on the tower roof!

In today's reality, how do we survive? What can helpless ordinary people do to stay healthy and sane? People drink bottled water, eat organic food, exercise, jog along polluted streets, and after all that, they say: "I am so tired, exhausted, restless. I need a vacation." Indeed! After two weeks in the mountains or by a lake far from the big city, you recharge your batteries, feel refreshed and strong. Even one weekend spent hiking or fishing can do so much good. How does it work? What is involved? A stress-free environment, plenty of fresh air, unadulterated oxygen, pure water, that's what. Did you notice how all your bright ideas come as oxygen invades your brain cells. Write down all those bright ideas because when you get back to the city, all is forgotten.

Look at our hard working farmers, and observe how well and healthy they are. Most of them don't put on tights and frequent the gym. They live simply in a healthy environment and consume fresh wholesome food. So what are we city folks doing to stay healthy and live longer? Well, use common sense, and ask your grandpa. Take two holidays instead of one long one, get out of town each weekend if you can, go for walks in the park, or along the river or lake, and be aware which way the wind blows the pollution. Avoid jogging on city streets in rush hours or you will inhale three times more pollution than in the evening when streets are almost traffic-free. Exercise regularly at home, in the garden, or on your balcony. It is not necessary to wear black tights and travel to a gymnasium to stay fit and healthy.

Eat discriminately, the less you eat, the better off you are...you are what you eat! Some people claim a vegetarian diet is most healthy, others compromise a bit and eat fish and chicken, as well. Still others feel there is no meal without steak. Who is right? Moderation and variety is the key. White meat is good, too much fat is not. Raw and steamed vegetables are the best, so is pasta with cheese. Tons of green salads, all types of fruit, are a must. Drink fruit and vegetable juices, milk, and water a total of eight glasses a day. Soft drinks containing sugar and addictive substances should be avoided, same with 'junk food', which is exactly just that, junk.

If you drink more than three cups of coffee, and smoke, you do not care for your health. Soon you may pay a high price, perhaps even with your life. You have a choice – you can enjoy a healthy life or you can die of cancer along with 43,000 Canadian smokers! Your physical health is one half of who you are – mental health is your other half. A positive, right attitude is 'it'. Avoid stress and conflict, be tolerant and accepting. Some people seem to relish arguing and fighting. Do not impose your ways on others and you certainly will avoid a lot of unnecessary strife and stress. Remember stress kills.

Remember we are who we are – change yourself, if you can, don't try to change others. Your mental state impacts directly on your physical shape. Someone compared a man to a car – long strenuous physical activities may be compared to a car being driven on high octane gas at 100km/h, it burns all clean in the engine. Climbing a mountain or running 10 km overhauls and cleanses your body so you feel healthy and vigorous. Moderation is advised, you should not run a marathon or climb Mt. Everest every day – a sustained moderately intensive exercise once or twice a week is good for you. If you choose to do it in the mountains, you get an extra bonus of fresh air and pure water. A healthy environment plus a healthy lifestyle equals a healthy, productive, and happy society. Life can be a dream, if we know how to live it up.

Did you plant some beautiful trees on your property lately? To live in the urban forest is certainly healthier than living in a polluted concrete jungle. Donate money to tree planting programs. Plant an oxygen-producing, beautiful tree today.

· PLATES ·

Above: L*ower Consolation Lake nestles in picturesque Consolation Valley, just below the Upper Lake, a short walk east of Moraine Lake. The photograph is taken from the slopes of Mt. Babel in September, when Larch trees turn yellow. In the background are the colourful slopes of Panorama Ridge (2824m) east of the Lake. Banff National Park.*

Left: T*he second half of September is the right time to visit Larch Valley, situated high above Moraine Lake. As the name implies, the valley is home to a large colony of Larches, which in the autumn turn bright yellow, then gold, then deep brown. By half of October strong winds shake the needles off. Heavily glaciated Mt. Fay (3234m) admiringly looks on and awaits the inevitable long winter. Banff National Park.*

Above: M*t. Wilson (3261m), a giant mountain stretching for 10km is comprised of several major peaks. The entire north side is heavily glaciated and the upper part is veiled with snow for most of the year. Here the northeast part basks in the gorgeous autumn morning light and colour. Banff National Park.*

Left: I*t cannot get any better than this, a perfect view of still Patricia Lake and snowy Pyramid Mountain (2766m) on a November morning. On the summit sits a large microwave transmitter, still in use. The mountain is a major landmark and tourist sight in the Jasper area. Jasper National Park.*

Upper: The fun of camping' can be a relative term. Camping by a lake in a camper, or large tent, full of supplies and goodies is definitely great fun. On the summit of Mt. Bourgeau (2930m), in the dead of winter with an austere -20°C, it can be a different story. One hopes to merely survive; on the other hand, the good news is: there are no mosquitoes at all. Lit by low morning sunlight is Mt. Brett (2984m) on the left and very rugged Pilot Mountain (2935m). Banff National Park.

Lower: A rare occurrence in the Rockies, from this high peak one can see flat bald Prairies with no foothills between. The view from Mt. Alderson (2692m) to the east is photographed at sunset. On the left is Mt. Crandell, in the centre Bertha Peak, all located in cozy, beautiful, rich in flora and fauna, Waterton Lakes National Park.

Upper: To escape summer's heat waves, some migrate to high country to cool off. Columbia Icefield is the ideal place to do that. Located in the southeast corner of Jasper National Park, it is not an easy place to access. No road, trail or path, just snow covered ice, full of hidden bottomless crevasses. Only well experienced and equipped parties should attempt such a trip. It is a base camp for climbing The Snow Dome, Kitchener, The Twins and Mt. Columbia.

Lower: Just north of the picturesque town of Field stands rugged Mt. Burgess (2599m). The summit offers a splendid view in all directions. Here looking south, the northwest end of Ottertail Range with lofty glaciated Mt. Vaux (3319m) can be admired. A moderate to difficult climb, this interesting peak is nearly 2200m high from base to summit. Yoho National Park.

Above: *A*n attractive campsite on the summit of Mt. Daly (3152m). The temperature hovers at -20°C on this crisp October morning around breakfast time. The sumptuous menu includes: snow melt water, noodles, dry vegetables and salami. The wide-angle lens covers the huge area to the southwest. A sharp eye will recognize: Mts. Stephen, Vaux, Wapta, King, Niles, Carnarvon and The President. Yoho National Park.

Left: *I*f there be paradise, this is it – a sweeping, incredible view from Ptarmigan Peak (3059m) to the northeast. The Skoki Lakes (Zigadenus and Myosotis) get their colour from the glacier below. Golden Larches drape Skoki Valley, north of Deception Pass. In centre left stands Skoki Mountain, to right of which is the source of the Red Deer River. Banff National Park.

Above: North *of Jasper National Park, sprawls a large pristine wilderness called Willmore Wilderness Park which harbours rich flora and fauna. Moose, Caribou, Grizzly and Wolf, are quite common residents here. Mighty Smoky River originates at Adolphus Lake and flows north to join the Peace River on its journey to the Arctic Ocean. Nearby, north of here, a devastating clear-cut logging operation threatens this fragile eco-system.*

Left: Seldom *is the mountain weather so kind to a photographer. September is known to be sunny with calm winds, pleasantly chilly day temperatures, and colder nights. Within ten days the path of still green poplars will turn into rich yellow-gold hues gloriously attiring Patricia Lake and Pyramid Mountain (2766m). Jasper National Park.*

Above: O*n the southeast peak of Odaray Mountain (3159m) looking south. On the left stands imposing Mt. Goodsir, in the middle foreground is glaciated Mt. Owen (3087m) and on the right horizon pointy white Mt. Vaux of the Ottertail Range can be seen. Access is via O'Hara Lake Road, then McArthur Pass, and west over the east slopes. Yoho National Park.*

Left: P*hotographed from the lesser southeast peak, Mt. Odaray (3159m) presents two obstacles in the form of short rock faces, preventing the solo climber from reaching the summit. The first face may be encircled to the south, the second must be ascended. On the right stands distant Cathedral Mountain (3189m), which presents several challenging climbing routes as well. Below Linda Lake can be seen. Yoho National Park.*

Upper: A large member of the Deer Family, the majestic Elk (Cervus elephus) is very common throughout the Rockies and wilderness areas west of here. It is July and plenty of gourmet food keeps the Elk healthy and happy. Their enormous showy antlers, still in velvet, will soon be ready for the rutting battles between contender bulls in early September.

Lower: The Grizzly Bear (Ursus arctos) is the undisputed monarch of the Canadian wilderness. Hunted and poached, its numbers are declining; only National Parks provide adequate protection for them. The Grizzly's tame look and slow movements are misleading. This is an extremely unpredictable animal, fast and dangerous, capable of killing just about any animal and humans.

Left: A moody picturesque scene by the Valley of the Ten Peaks near Moraine Lake. Mt. Babel (3101m) and the other high peaks are excellent weather makers. This is the Great Divide area where rain is plentiful, thus valleys and meadows are lush and green. August is the time to see these gorgeous flowers. Banff National Park.

Herbert Lake is a small in size body of water, but very big in beauty. Here many high peaks of the Lake Louise area can be viewed; from the left are Mt. Temple, Fairview, and Aberdeen. The lake nestles along the scenic Jasper Highway just northwest of Lake Louise. Banff National Park.

Along Rockies' east slopes in the Kananaskis, many spectacular sights can be admired. One of them is Mt. Kidd (2958m), right peak being the higher, reflected in small tarn along Kananaskis River. West, north and east approaches are for climbers. Southeast gully between two peaks is a nice scramble route.

Above: Rainbows are quite common in rainy places. Here at the confluence of the Bow and Spray Rivers in Banff, a rare double ribbon of vivid colour adorns Mt. Rundle on a rainy July afternoon. It is amazing that the photo taken through heavy, nearly down-pouring rain, came out this sharp. An old cliché comes to mind: be in the right place, at the right time and one gets a great shot.

Left: Hmm, what lake is that? Looks like reversed Peyto Lake. Indeed, the lake is viewed from a less visited viewpoint – Caldron Peak (2917m) located southwest of the lake. Hazy summer morning background is provided by Observation Peak (3174m) to the north and below it the Jasper-Lake Louise Highway can be seen. Banff National Park.

At the south end of Paradise Valley, looming above Horseshoe Glacier, Hungabee Mountain (3493m) is located. Climbing any route here is mostly 'treacherous' and recommended only for top guns. First ascended by H.C. Parker lead by two guides in 1903. This view is from the summit of Mt. Temple (3543m) on a bright, very cold and crisp September morning. All one can say is "Wow, what a view". Banff National Park.

At the south end of Waputik Icefield, Mt. Daly (3152m) stands guard. Bivouacking here in October is not exactly fun, but a photo such as this is ample reward. Bronzed by the setting sun is the southwest face of Mt. Balfour (3272m), the dominant point of Waputik Range. The following morning brought a bone chilling -20°C temperature, but also great conditions for fine photography and sightseeing. Yoho National Park.

Above: Man-made but picturesque Barrier Lake on Kananaskis River provides electric power, water sports, fishing and fine scenery. First autumn snow blanketed the valley, richly decorating yellow poplars and shrubs. The snow won't last long as October gets warm and sunny days called 'Indian summer', but after that white will dominate the scene for over six months.

Left: Geraldine Valley in Jasper National Park is blessed with several large lakes and waterfalls. Early summer is the best time to see the roaring white waters. August presents a wide variety of alpine flowers. Common in the Valley, the wildlife includes: Grizzly Bear, Goat, Wolf, and occasionally Mountain Caribou, to name a few major species.

Above: $\mathcal{B}$*ivouacking on upper slopes of Mt. Hector (3394m) is convenient for next morning's dash for the summit. Mt. Hector is one of these mountains, which can be climbed quite easily, summer or winter, and being quite high provides excellent scenery in all directions. One can only hope that this boulder won't move for a while. Banff National Park.*

Left: $\mathcal{C}$*ome late September the Larch Valley above Moraine Lake turns into a Mecca for nature lovers. Large groves of Larch trees turn into bright yellow, then golden, and after several frigid nights and strong October winds, the needles are shaken off and the winter in the high country is around the corner. It will take nearly eight months before life returns to the Valley. Banff National Park.*

A breathtaking view, towards the east, from Ptarmigan Peak (3059m). On the left is Baker Lake, the right horizon is dominated by three peaks of Bonnet Peak (3235m) of the Sawback Range. This rather rough and tortured but fascinating landscape is photographed at late September sunset. Banff National Park.

East of Wonder Pass (2425m), Wonder Peak (2852m) overlooks Marvel Lake to the south. The view presented here is to the southwest featuring Mt. Aye on the left, Mt. Assiniboine (3618m) at centre, and incredibly rugged world just west of Wonder Pass. While pests like Grizzlies or mosquitoes reside in the valleys, the author bivouacks safely on the mountains.

Above: Most of us are accustomed to looking at Mt. Rundle from Banff. This 'different' shot is photographed from the east and offers a less well known view – a wintry Mt. Rundle (2998m). This range-like mountain is nearly 15km in length, starts in Banff and terminates south of Canmore. First ascended by known solo climber, J.J. McArthur, in 1888, it has become quite popular with scramblers and climbers since then. The entire traverse can be done in two days or, if all goes well, in one long day. Banff National Park.

Left: How stark, not wanting to say 'ugly', can mountains get. Except for a little green path of trees in the centre, all is gray and grayer. This gray giant on the left is Mt. Sir Douglas (3406m), at centre Mt. Robertson (3194m) and on the right towers Mt. French (3234m). Below them to the south sprawls large Haig Glacier obscured by front peaks. All that rugged beauty is viewed from the summit of Mt. Worthington (2838m), which looms above Three Isle Lake in Kananaskis Country.

Above: The fame of the fabulous beauty of the Valley of the Ten Peaks, reaches far beyond the Rockies. The area is blessed with more great features in one small area than any other is: emerald Moraine Lake, sharp lofty peaks, glaciers, swift creeks, and verdant lively flora and fauna. The Grizzly Bear is at home here, which causes some concern. Grizzlies and hikers do not mix well. Group hiking and caution is always advised. Banff National Park.

Left: Autumnal Blakiston Creek Valley in windy Waterton Lakes National Park is known for its variety of vegetation, providing forage for a number of game species: Deer, Elk, Moose, Grizzly Bear, Black Bear and Sheep frequent the area regularly. Coyote, Cougar, Lynx,Wolf, Wolverine and Badger, may be seen as well. On the left is Ruby Ridge (2436m), on the right stands the apex of Waterton Park - Mt. Blakiston (2910m).

Above: A *sweeping view of endless mountains unfolds from the summit of Mt. Richardson (3086m). On the left is Lake Marlin, in the middle is the Wall of Jericho, and on the right horizon looms Mt. Douglas and Mt. St. Bride. Mt. Richardson is located 9km northeast of Lake Louise and west of Pika Peak and is easily accessible from Hidden Lake via south ridge. Banff National Park.*

Left: O*verwhelmingly beautiful and moody are high vistas viewed from a lofty peak. No matter how many times one climbs high, the enchantment and discovery continue. Each day is different as are one's feelings and impressions. Here we look south towards flamboyant Mt. Assiniboine from equally interesting Storm Mountain (3161m) of the Ball Range. Kootenay/Banff National Parks.*

The winter ascent of Mt. Thompson (3065m) affords this fine but slightly hazy view of Wapta Icefield to the southeast. In the middle ground-right is pointed little St. Nicholas Peak (2970m), above it to the left is Mt. Olive (3130m) behind which is Vulture Pass (2932m), the route to Balfour Pass and Hut via the Vulture Glacier. Directly above, the horizon is dominated by huge Mt. Balfour (3272m); Mt. Gordon is off the photo on the right. Banff National Park.

If you enjoy a very long, toilsome, endless, walk up - Sunwapta Peak (3315m) is the place. Located 6km north of Tangle Ridge and 15km northeast of Mt. Alberta, it is a huge, long ridge-like mountain between Jonas Creek and Sunwapta River and offers interesting views in all directions – including this one to the east. To the northwest Mt. Brazeau is only 23km away, Mt. Columbia, The Twins and Alberta are seen, and huge white pyramid of Mt. Clemenceau graces the southwestern horizon. Jasper National Park.

*Above: A*n early morning hike to Fairview Mountain (2744m) is well rewarded. A splendid sunrise richly illuminates glaciated Mt. Victoria (3464m). Part of Mt. Lefroy is visible on the left. This is an easy pleasant hike south of Lake Louise via the Saddle and offers rewarding views in all directons. Banff National Park.

Left: A flamboyant and lofty Mt. Erebus (3119m) and its challenging north ridge. Eremite Glacier on the left and Simon Valley on the right. The right horizon is dominated by massive Mt. Mastodon (2987m). Photographed from Outpost Peak (2865m), located on the south side of Tonquin Valley. Jasper National Park.

Above: *G*lacier-carved Consolation Valley, Lower and Upper Consolation Lakes, are a short pleasant walk from Moraine Lake. The Panorama Ridge is on the left-east, Mt. Babel to the west, and glacier clad Mt. Quadra flanks the valley on the south. The splendid scene was photographed from the Tower of Babel (2360m). Banff National Park.

Left: *A* grand view from a small mountain. Mt. Schaffer (2692m) is in reality a northwest ridge of Mt. Biddle. The photo features the northeast view encompassing Mary and O'Hara Lakes, Wiwaxy Peak on the left, Mt. Huber (3368m) in the centre, and behind is a long ridge of Mt. Victoria. This is a real climber's paradise. Yoho National Park.

Above: The *Pyramid Mountain (2766m) and Lake need no introduction. A prime landmark of the town of Jasper seen here at its best. Veiled in first November snow, early morning light brings out all physical features and colour. A pleasant inspiring sight, a reward for the early riser. Jasper National Park.*

Left: R*eflected in mirror-like Maligne Lake is the sun-bronzed Leah Peak (2801m). The large spectacular and still pristine Maligne Lake is flanked on both sides by high wild mountains, the far end is graced by the apex of the Maligne Group – Mt. Brazeau and its icefield (not on photo). Jasper National Park.*

Above: The jewel of the Rockies – Bow Lake, is located just east of the Great Divide. Behind this Crowfoot Mountain (3050m) sprawls immense Wapta Icefield and one of its many glaciers – Bow Glacier gives birth to the Bow River. The river drains southern Alberta, joins the South Saskatchewan River and empties into Hudson's Bay and Atlantic Ocean.

Left: November 18, 2001 an intense meteorite shower was forecasted. This 20 minute exposure captured three of these meteorites and also caught some of the Northern Lights and Polaris, around which stars 'circle' as the earth rotates. Jagged peaks add extra flavour to the mountain photo, exposed at 2:00 a.m. on a very cold night by Medicine Lake. Jasper National Park.

Above: A*nytime is a good time to climb Mt. Hector (3394m), even winter would do. Relatively easy to access and technically not too difficult. Five or six hours of a little workout through dense forest, alps, scree, snow and ice, will reward one with a 'WOW' view of emerald Hector Lake, Waputik Range with Mt. Balfour to the west. The south view is every bit as attractive. Banff National Park.*

Left: I*s it worth climbing Mt. Worthington (2838m)? Some say, yes. The author nearly died of hypothermia on that cold, snowy peak, a long time ago. After learning his mountain lore, he lately enjoyed the climb. From Upper Kananaskis Lake, go west to Three Isle Lake. Easy access of the mountain is from the west or south sides. In late autumn the lake is half empty, the east flowing Three Isle Creek joins Kananaskis River.*

Just next to the Trans-Canada Highway and picturesque town of Field, Mt. Stephen (3199m) stands tall. Although the west ridge on the right looks smooth and easy, it is not. The last part is very jagged, broken and razor sharp. The author gained a great deal of mountain lore on that ridge, so much so that on the way back he took a southeast route, which turned out not to be easier at all. Yoho National Park is a small Park but is loaded with unusual visual and natural features like Takakkaw Falls, Wapta Falls, Emerald Lake, hoodoos, glaciers and icefields.

Columbia Icefield area is rich in photographic subjects; great photographic opportunities await the cameraman year round. Take a short hike off the road and discover much more. If you are a hardy hiker, scrambler or experienced mountaineer, a real world of adventure is yours. Climb Mt. Wilcox, Nigel, go higher to Athabasca or ultimately climb into the Columbia Icefield…where blizzards and whiteouts can last for seven days. Mt. Athabasca on the left, Andromeda on the right, fast-melting Athabasca Glacier below. Jasper National Park.

Above: T*he Tonquin Valley is a place like no other. Two Amethyst Lakes are fed by water from snow and ice of The Ramparts, a beautiful jagged range 15km long. The lakes give birth to a fine whitewater Astoria River. The Valley's rich vegetation supports a variety of wildlife – Mountain Caribou and the Grizzly being the most attractive. Meadows here are a flowery paradise, which includes the showy blue Lupine. Southeast of here the mighty Fraser River has its source. Jasper National Park.*

Left: M*t. Assiniboine Provincial Park, with all these incredible natural features, should have been upgraded to National Park status a long time ago, for maximum protection. This miniature park houses eleven lakes, twelve major mountains, some glaciers, and the Mitchell River originates here. But above all, Mt. Assiniboine (3618m), the sixth highest mountain of the Rockies, looms here sky high challenging top climbers. The mountain was discovered in 1885 and several attempts were made to climb it. Sixteen years later in 1901, J. Outram with two guides, set foot on this lofty twin peak mountain for the first time. Elizabeth Lake is in the foreground, the next is Cerulean Lake.*

Above: A *close-up look at Mt. Victoria located between Lake Louise and Lake O'Hara. The main south summit (3464m) is in the centre left, lesser North Peak (3388m) in centre right. On the right, part of Mt. Collier is visible. This beautiful alpine mountain is a well-known and admired landmark. J.N. Collie and C.E. Fay first scaled the mountain in 1897, with two guides. Banff National Park.*

Left: A *t the far end of Chephren Lake, flamboyant and lofty Howse Peak (3290m) stands guard, and is the highest summit of the Waputik Group. No easy route here. Approach from the southwest via Howse River requires a 28km walk in, climbing northeast face (photo) is rated as very severe (5.7/F7). Five climbers via west, northwest route completed first ascent in 1902. Banff National Park.*

Above: *F*ascinating but feared by all, humans and beasts alike, the Grizzly Bear (Ursus arctos) is a force to be reckoned with. A member of the Ursidae Family, the Grizzly is classified as 'dish-faced' to distinguish it from the seven other groups of bears. Coloration of this omnivorous predator ranges from light tawny, to brown, to deep reddish. Some say the Grizzly is merely a regional variation in colour and size of Alaska's Kodiak.

Left: *A* magnificent close-up of emerald-green Skoki Lakes (Zigadenus, larger; Myosotis, smaller). Located just west of Deception Pass at the north base of Ptarmigan Peak (3059m) from where the photo was taken. The icy water flows north via Skoki Valley to join Little Pipestone Creek. The rock flour and glacial silt are responsible for the water's emerald colour, as the autumn frost is for the golden colour of Larch trees. Banff National Park.

The east face of Mt. Athabasca (3490m) viewed from Hilda Creek angle. Banff/Jasper National Parks. Located along the scenic Jasper Highway, an eastern sentinel of the Columbia Icefield, the mountain is favoured by many climbers. The author scaled it solo four times, including a winter ascent. First ascended by J.N. Collie and H. Woolley in 1898 who were the first to discover Columbia Icefield.

One of many towers of Mt. Wilson (3261m), a huge mountain located by the Jasper Highway, northwest of the confluence of the North Saskatchewan, Mistaya and Howse Rivers. A major body of ice sprawls on the north slopes. The entire area is a major Mountain Goat habitat. First ascended by J. Outram guided by C. Kaufmann in 1902. Banff National Park.

Above: The light reveals real character and name of the place – the Sawback Range. The low light of the setting sun richly bronzes this exceptionally rugged part of the range west of Banff. The range begins just northwest of Banff and continues northwest for nearly 40km, terminating at the Red Deer River. Banff National Park.

Left: The 1875m high, perpendicular northwest face of Mt. Stephen (3199m) is often called "treacherous" and rightly so. A very challenging, but pleasant, climb via several routes. On the summit, there is a large microwave station. The photo was taken from Mt. Burgess across the valley to the northwest. Yoho National Park.

Above: Hoary Marmot (Marmota eligata) *belongs to a group of large terrestrial squirrels – Marmota. Quite common throughout the Canadian Rockies, they live on alpine meadows above the tree line and rely on large boulders and rock slides for safety. Each colony has a senior sentry on watch and when danger approaches, the sentry sounds a sharp loud shrill warning.*

Left: The *sub-alpine tundra surrounds the Bow Lake near the source of the Bow River. The hardy, yet showy, Fireweed (Epilobium angustifolium) grows in diversified regions from the low valleys to alpine meadows, as high as 2500m. The mountain in the background is the northern peak of Crowfoot Mountain (3050m). Bow Lake sprawls just behind these trees. Banff National Park.*

Above: On the way to Citadel Pass (2362m) and Mt. Assiniboine, large lush meadows sprawl in the valleys. A variety of wild flowers and plants is astonishing here, so is the wildlife. Distant left horizon features Mt. Brett and Mt. Bourgeau; on the right is sprawling Mt. Howard Douglas (2820m). Boundary of Kootenay and Banff National Parks along the Great Divide.

Left: In early summer when snow melts quickly, all small creeks look like large rivers. This weeping wall is called Tangle Falls and is just off the Jasper Highway west of Columbia Icefield. The area is very snowy and provides plenty of water in early summer's run-off. In late autumn almost all that water dries up resulting in no falls. Jasper National Park.

Above: A serene view of the Bow River just east of Canmore. From the left is Mt. Grassi (2684m), Ha Ling Peak (2680m) is next, Canmore Gap, and the east end of Mt. Rundle. All these peaks have many fine climbing routes of various difficulties. The Bow River provides the splendid late autumn foreground.

Left: The southeast face of Odaray Mountain (3159m) as seen from Mt. Schaffer. Mt. Odaray is located 3km west of Lake O'Hara with easy ascent from McArthur Pass, turning northwest, gaining southeast ridge. Near the summit a deep chimney and rock face will prevent most amateur climbers from reaching the summit. Yoho National Park.

Above: Along the Lake Louise-Jasper road, just east of Bow Summit, the picturesque Bow Lake is nestled among high glaciated peaks. The Bow River originates at Bow Glacier south of here. The area is a year-round mountaineering paradise. The major route entering Wapta Icefield begins here and leads into several mountain huts and several mountains to be scaled: Mt. Crowfoot, St. Nicholas, Gordon, Thompson, and a few others. Banff National Park.

Left: A long, long time ago when the author was young and daring, not to mention foolish, he made two solo ascents of The President (3138m). The first climb ended in total disaster when he stepped on a large crevasse covered by a new drift of snow, and only miraculously avoided falling in. Upon reaching the summit, the weather closed in, snow fell, and no photos would be taken. The second climb, a week later, brought extremely cold, but splendid, October weather, at which time a few pictures were taken. Both ascents were made via Little Yoho Valley, Emerald Glacier and Pass via southwest ridge. Yoho National Park.

Above: Several hundred years ago the entire Prairies were populated by millions of Buffalo or Bison *(Bison bison). As the settling of the region progressed, nearly all of these impressive animals were hunted down. Today only a few herds remain in National Parks and private reserves, hopefully assuring the survival of this fascinating great beast.*

Left: As a poet said: "beauty is everywhere for those who can and want to see it". Here a humble little plant – Goat's Beard illuminated by the setting sun, revealing all of its delicate sparkling details and intricate patterns which nature has so meticulously created. While climbing a mountain is a physical accomplishment, taking close-up photos of nature is a creative feat, as well as great fun.

Above: The Tower of Babel (2360m) is a buttress of the long north ridge of Mt. Babel, located southeast of Moraine Lake. A genuine rock climbing paradise on good quartzite. Several major climbing routes lead to this small but interesting summit. The southeast face of bulky Mt. Temple (3543m) is just across the valley to the northwest (photo). Banff National Park.

Left: At the upper end of Larch Valley between Mt. Temple and Eiffel Peak, Pinnacle Mountain (3067m) stands guard. As the name implies, it is just that, a pinnacle, not easy to access. J.W.A. Hickson ascended it for the first time in 1909 with two guides. Several climbing routes lead to the summit of this torturous and difficult mountain. Banff National Park.

Above: A *seldom seen occurrence, which happens every month, year round. Simultaneous sunrise and moonset on Mt. Victoria (3464m) by the west end of Lake Louise. The day before or day later, the moon is too high in the sky or already set – gone at sunrise. The cloudy skies or just a few clouds in the wrong place often prevent us from seeing this fascinating phenomenon. Banff National Park.*

Left: O*nly in September when days are sunny and the air is dry can such a crisp sharp photo be captured. Sunrise on the summit of Mt. Athabasca (3490m) looking southwest. The foreground features the bright east glacier of Mt. Andromeda and the middle ground features Mt. Castleguard (3077m), the southeast apex of the Columbia Icefield. (Banff/Jasper National Parks. Three peaks of giant Mt. Bryce (3507m) located outside National Park dominate the horizon, the right (west) peak being the highest.*

Emerald Lake is a splendid wonder of the Rockies. Being just west of the Continental Divide the area gets enough precipitation to sustain healthy, green vegetation and forest. Wildlife is plentiful as animals find gourmet dining here. Emerald Lake is accessible by road year round; tourist facilities do exist here; water sports are at its best, but above all the scenery is breathtaking. Yoho National Park.

Yellowhead Mtn. (2412m) resembles Sawback Range, with many jagged peaks and stretches for several kilometres. Reflected here in mirror-like Witney Lake, it is located in the eastern part of Mt. Robson Provincial Park. This is Moose country; it is not unusual to see three or five Moose in the area, especially early in the morning. A hungry Wolf is lurking behind bushes, waiting for a young or weak animal.

Above: A classic sunrise witnessed from Cascade Mountain (2998m) just north of Banff townsite. Richly illuminated with colourful hues of sunrise, a great panorama of jagged peaks unfolds – looking west. At the right foreground is the eastern face of Mt. Louis, middle ground right –centre features Pilot Mountain, and on the central horizon looms the ice-covered great pyramid of Mt. Ball. Banff National Park.

Left: The western sentinel of the Columbia Icefield, the North Twin (3683m) is the third highest elevation in the Rockies, after Mt. Robson and Mt. Columbia. This splendid sunrise is photographed from Woolley Shoulder. To gain access from Jasper Road, the icy Sunwapta River must be forded, followed by a long bushwack Once above tree line, find the way through the upper valley. Most laborious is the steep scramble on snowy Woolley Shoulder, but the breathtaking view that awaits, is worth all your efforts. Jasper National Park.

Above: Lake O'Hara and Mary Lake, the shining jewels of Yoho National Park, are featured and described on page 52. Repeating this photo illustrates clearly how "rock flour" and glacial silt affects the colour of the lake. Both photos were taken on an early September morning in different years, and what a contrast in colour. Take four photos in four months of this lake and you get four different colours.

Left: Climbing Mt. Edith Cavell (3363m) four times without getting one quality photo is more than frustrating. That also includes the author bivouacking on the summit three times. Snow storms, whiteouts as clouds hang over the summit, are the order of the day here – this mountain creates its own weather. The 'ugly' photo features the northwest view. Angel Glacier is in the centre, Cavell Lake on the right, below it Astoria River is visible. Jasper National Park.

A *great, clear crisp morning always allows one to produce a quality photo. Regretfully one can only be in one location as the sunrise's colour lasts for a mere 20-30 seconds. This is the east face of Pilot Mtn. (2935m) located just south of Highway 1 and Redearth Creek. The mountain presents a moderately difficult scramble. The exposed chimney below the summit is icy in early summer, thus dangerous. Banff National Park.*

The ultimate north wall of renowned Mt. Edith Cavell (3363m) basks in the gorgeous mid-summer morning sun. First ascended in 1915 from the south by Gilmour-Holaway team. Many climbing routes have been established since. The north face (photo) climb can be done in one day if conditions allow. It is a 1200m climb on quartzite, 55-60° steep ice, snow and extremely dangerous shale. Jasper National Park.

Above: T*he formidably beautiful north side of Mt. Robson (3954m) and Berg Lake as seen from the north – high ridge west of Toboggan Creek. On the left is Berg Glacier and above it stands The Helmet (3401m); on the right side of the mountain is treacherous Emperor Ridge and Misty Glacier is on the right. The Robson Glacier east of here provides most of the water for Berg Lake, which is the beginning of the Robson River on which several large falls, Emperor Falls, being the highest can be seen. Mt. Robson Provincial Park.*

Left: I*s this Moraine Lake, some will ask? Yes, indeed it is, as seen from the Tower of Babel (2360m). Along the wall of the "Ten Peaks", Wenkchemna Glacier is visible, covered by gravel and fallen rock. In the middle of the skyline is Wenkchemna Pass (2600m) allowing access to Prospectors Valley and Lake O'Hara via Opabin Pass. On the right is Eiffel Peak and behind the top of Wenkchemna Peak, peak number ten is seen. Banff National Park.*

Above: M*t. Foch (3180m) offers splendid views in all directions. Located just south of Upper Kananaskis Lake it belongs to the Joffre Group. The misty morning photo features Upper and Lower Kananaskis Lakes, Kananaskis Range on the left and Opal Range on the right. To get there is not by hiking but rather a difficult scramble or climb, with the easiest access being from Upper Elk Lake via south slopes and the east ridge. The west ridge from Sorrail-Foch Col may even be easier.*

Left: T*he Nub Peak (2748m) is a southeast ridge of Nestor Peak located just north of the Park's boundary. The Nub is a hill north of Cerulean Lake and offers great views of the entire Mt. Assiniboine area. Early winter mountaineering in this remote region is the real thing. To reach here from the north or east is over 20km and takes a full day. Mt. Assiniboine (3618m), also called the Canadian Matterhorn, the sixth highest mountain of the Rockies, looms tall in the centre.*

99

Above: Spring has arrived at the Third Vermilion Lake just west of Banff. The Lake, one of three, nestles in a large marshy area along the Bow River and, despite being in the vicinity of a busy tourist centre, the eco-system appears to be fairly healthy. All aquatic creatures and waterfowl find adequate habitat here, even a pair of Bald Eagle and Osprey call it their summer home. Banff National Park.

Left: At the west end of Larch Valley above Moraine Lake, Eiffel Peak (3084m) dominates the area. It is an easy scramble from the trail to Eiffel Lake. The summit offers a splendid view of the entire Valley of the Ten Peaks, Paradise Valley, Pinnacle Mountain, Mt. Temple, Lefroy, and many others. The area on both sides of Wenkchemna Pass is a permanent home to Grizzly Bears – there have been a few 'bear incidents' here. Extra caution is advised. Banff National Park.

Above: It *may look like aerial photography, but it is not. The author, being a mountain man, would never resort to that method – he climbs mountains instead. In order to capture this morning low light and mist, he bivouacked on the summit of Mt. Temple (3543m) and attained this reward. Mt. Assiniboine dominates the horizon, on the left is Consolation Valley and Pass above which Storm Mountain is visible. On the right horizon, the white dome of Mt. Ball and its northern extension Stanley Peak is seen. Mt. Quadra and Mt. Babel are prominent on the right foreground – a high paradise of first magnitude. Banff National Park.*

Left: "S*omewhere over the rainbow…"the huge Takakkaw Falls (Native Canadian for 'splendid') spills its icy waters down to the Yoho River. The total drop is over 300m, the water comes from the Daly Glacier of Waputik Icefield to the east. The ideal time to view this spectacle is in early summer when the snow and ice is melting rapidly. Yoho National Park.*

Above: The*re is only one rainforest in the fairly dry Rockies and it happens to be situated near the Rockies' highest peak – Mt. Robson (3954m). Lofty mountains 'catch' clouds passing by and consequently get plenty of rain and snow. The trees are tall, the forest floor dense with lush bush and brushwood, and the area is very verdant. These excellent 'dining facilities' invite all species of wildlife to a feast. Mt. Robson Provincial Park.

Left: The* same story as above applies here. The great Fraser River begins high up north of Fraser Pass, 15km south of Mt. Fraser in the general area south of Tonquin Valley. The high glacier-clad mountains provide plenty of rock flour and silt, which gives the water its emerald green colour. The Fraser flows northwest and at Prince George winds to the south, drains central British Columbia, and empties into the Pacific Ocean by Vancouver. Mt. Robson Provincial Park.

Above: H*alf way between Banff and Lake Louise guarding the Bow Valley stands the well-know landmark – Castle Mountain (2766m). The Bow River is awakening after a long winter break. Six months of harsh winter is coming to an end and in the next few weeks, the river will come alive with scores of waterfowl. The Osprey and Bald Eagle will fish and so the fish will be the element of that eternal chain of life. Banff National Park.*

Left: E*merald Lake is the shining jewel of Yoho National Park, accessible by road year round. Wintry Mt. Burgess (2599m) reflects its sun-bronzed northwest face in the half-frozen lake as spring begins its arrival. A major habitat for Moose, Loon and other waterfowl. The flora and scenery is at its best here.*

Above: The Aurora Borealis or Northern Lights are without a doubt the most elusive subject for the photographer to capture, unless one lives near the Arctic Circle. The Latin word 'Aurora" means dawn, a luminous celestial phenomenon of magnetic character occurring in the Polar region of the north. The very same nocturnal show occurs in the southern Antarctic Circle region and is called 'Aurora Australis' – Southern Lights. This unusually colourful display graced by a setting moon was photographed north of Lake Louise in May 2001.

Right: This patented classic photo is 30 years old, but has lost none of its refined gentle beauty. The birth of a glorious autumn day is witnessed from the summit of Storm Mountain (3161m). The mountain was first climbed in 1889 and remains popular with both scramblers and climbers ever since that time. Kootenay/ Banff National Parks.

Above: $\mathcal{M}$aligne Lake and the surrounding area is a magnificent and truly pristine wilderness in existence because of the protective aegis of the National Park. The lower part of the lake is accessible by road, thus damage is inflicted to a degree, but deeper in towards the lake where not even hiking trails exist, the area's natural beauty is in evidence. Let us hope we shall keep it that way. Jasper National Park.

Left: $\mathcal{T}$he majestic Mt. Chephren or Black Pyramid (3266m) shrouded in the white veil of the first autumn snow, turns its eastern face to the unusually serene waters of Lower Waterfowl Lake. First ascended in 1913 by J.W.A. Hickson guided by E. Feuz. The few routes leading to the summit are classified as 'hard'. The only scramble via the southeast gully encounters a difficult grade. Banff National Park.

*Above: N*umerous times in the past the author has climbed a high mountain only to realize when reaching the top that the air is full of ash particles blown from the west. This phenomenon is as a result of loggers in British Columbia burning slush and unused parts of trees on a massive scale. This disaster to nature was photographed east of Jasper, with Mt. Edith Cavell in the centre. The photo is taken on low grain film but looks as though fast grainy film was used, with no filter. Jasper National Park.

*Left: T*he one and only – Lake Louise – beautiful, colourful, scenic and wonderful. A major tourist attraction visited and admired by most comers to the Rockies. One may come here every day at sunrise only to find different light and colour. This would be a great shot if only the water was still. When the hot summer sun bounces off the wall of Mt. Victoria (3464m), air turbulence ensues, causing wind and, thus, not perfect reflections. Banff National Park.

*Above: A*t the southwest end of Paradise Valley, large Horseshoe Glacier sits at the foot of Hungabee Mountain. The glacial meltwater gives life to Paradise Creek, which tumbles and cascades down the steep valley. One of the major cataracts here is called the Giant Steps. The most opportune time to see this spectacle is in July when ice melting is profuse. Banff National Park.

*Left: T*he Mistaya River Valley nestles seven fairly large lakes, whose emerald waters came from glaciers and snow along the Great Divide. At the top is Caldron Lake, next is Peyto Lake, Mistaya, Cirque, Upper and Lower Waterfowl and Chephren. This photo taken from the knoll just east of Totem Creek features Lower Waterfowl Lake, and hidden at the foot of Howse Peak – Chephren Lake. Banff National Park.

Above: The apex of Waterton Lakes National Park – Mt. Blakiston (2910m) presents its stark craggy eastern face, richly bronzed by the rising Prairie sun. First ascended in 1942 from the north side (not an easy climb). A moderate scramble will access the summit, using the south side via Lineham Lakes Trail.

Left: Marshy swamps along the Kicking Horse River represent a major wildlife habitat. All water critters and those who try to feed on them make a decent living here. The unusually colourful sunset rays kiss the high peaks of the north end of Ottertail Range with lofty Mt. Vaux (3319m) on the left and Chancellor Peak (3280m) on the right. Yoho National Park.

Upper: *The quintessential mountain Mt. Alberta (3619m). Few people have seen, and fewer climbed this remote, difficult mountain. Viewed from Woolley Shoulder at sunrise, this is the fifth elevation of the Canadian Rockies. First climbed in 1925. Jasper National Park.*

Lower: *Richly bronzed by rising sun is the north ridge of Mt. Alderson on the left and gentle dome of Mt. Carthew at centre witnessed from the summit of Mt. Alderson (2692m). The Montana Rockies are only three kilometres to the south. Waterton Lakes National Park.*

*Upper: H*igh in the Vermilion Range along the unnamed "Rock Wall" (3045m) the picturesque Floe Lake nestles in peace. The area is accessible by a good trail from Radium Hwy in 4-5 hours. Viewed at sunrise from the north. Kootenay National Park.

*Lower: T*wo kilometres west of Deception Pass (2475m), Ptarmigan Peak (3059m) looms sky high. Glorious sunrise witnessed from the summit looking northwest. From the left is Mt. Richardson, Pika Peak and Mt. Hector at right. Banff National Park.

Along the high peaks of the Continental Divide, weather may be quite capricious and unpredictable: overcast, rainy or windy. This is one of those days at Moraine Lake, moody and pretty. Banff National Park.

Is it all black at night? With a large moon and snow white mountains, this 20-minute exposure more resembles a sunny day than a dark night. East end of The Valley of the Ten Peaks, beautiful. Banff National Park.

Above: *A*long the Foothills, east of the Rockies, summer thunderstorms are a common occurrence. These are the result of highly electrified clouds and are often associated with heavy rain. The discharge of that power occurs in a flash, or very large spark, which we call lightning. Lightning may target another cloud or the earth. Many people are injured or killed every year by these illusive and spectacular, but sometimes deadly thunderstorms.

Left: *C*aused by giant electrical storms in the upper atmosphere, the mysterious Aurora Borealis performs its sinuous dance quickly or slowly, depending on the intensity of solar winds. The best time to view this mesmerizing northern phenomenon is from October to March when nights are long and dark; anywhere near the circumpolar region. Here, an extra bonus, Comet Hale Bopp soars over Jasper's Pyramid Mountain (2766m). Jasper National Park. Also see page 106.

Above: The fascinating scenery of Mt. Assiniboine area viewed from Sundance Range looking west. On the left, Mt. Gloria (2908m), hidden behind is Eon Mountain. Mt. Aye (3243m) is in the centre. Mt. Assiniboine (3618m) looms on the right, while over its left (south) shoulder hangs a little knoll called Lunette Peak (3400m). Marvel Lake most certainly marvels at its glorious surroundings – a beautiful lush forest teeming with wildlife and these magnificent lofty mountains. The mighty Grizzly Bear is at home here, while we are only visitors. On the left is a mid-winter image of the formidable northeast face of Mt. Assiniboine (3618m) basking in a glorious sunrise. Mt. Assiniboine Provincial Park/Banff National Park.

Above: Light, *better yet, unusual light make this photo. The morning sun backlit the mist over partially frozen Maligne Lake. In contrast the dark snowy silhouette of Unwin-Charlton Massif watches silently by the west shore. This large body of moving water may stay open and ice-free until early December, but will remain frozen until mid June. Jasper National Park.*

Left: What *could be more romantic than a full silvery moon hovering over snow-clad lofty peaks and reflected in spectacular Maligne Lake. Night photos are always high on the author's agenda and are most pleasurable. The only problem is that the moon rises in a different location each month. You may set yourself at the lake, but the moon may appear in a very difficult, unphotogenic place. Jasper National Park.*

Above: I*f this is not a "Rhapsody in Blue", what is? The Grassi Hut named after famous early mountaineer, Lawrence Grassi, stands at the southwest flank of Clemenceau Icefield, which is the western extension of Columbia Icefield. The author spent a marvellous week here in the dead of winter and literally went 'berserk' with his camera. Above the hut stands distant Mt. Clemenceau (3658m), the fourth highest elevation in the Rockies. On the right is the white pyramid of Tusk Peak (3340m), all gently lit by silvery quarter moon in this ten-minute exposure image.*

Left: A*t the low end of Peyto Glacier is situated a well-hidden ice cave entrance. One summer it may be large and visible, the next year it is small or totally gone. As the glacier recedes, the crevasses close tightly or open wide. Thus, spelunking in an ice cave may be hazardous to your life. The solid ice ceiling may suddenly open up and tons of ice come crashing down. Mountains are gorgeous in photographs but in cold reality they can be unforgiving, dangerous or downright deadly. Always play it safe and wise. Banff National Park.*

From Waterfowl Lakes take a trail south to Cirque Lake. Follow west shore south, climb steep slope west, reach the col, descend northwest towards Chephren Lake. Here is incredible scenery and the lake, but the weather turned bad. Descend steep moraine, follow the rugged east shore for three kilometres, then join the trail. In the background are many peaks of Mt. Murchison. Banff National Park.

Kootenay National Park is the most green, wild and pristine of the five Rocky Mountain National Parks. One can drive for a long while seeing no development, but verdant healthy forest, clear pure rivers and plenty of wildlife, especially in the spring and autumn. Large herds of wintering Elk can be seen as well. That is how all national parks should be. Reflected in a tarn along Vermilion River are peaks of Mitchell Range.

Above: J*asper's Pyramid Mountain (2766m) is just a short scramble from Pyramid Lake. In four or five hours, you can see this southwest vista and many more in all directions. Even lofty Mt. Robson may be clearly visible. Why do we climb? Youngsters do it for the physical challenge; as we mature we want to expand our horizons in more than just a physical way. Some climbers actually discover and admire the severe stark beauty of the heights. Climbing builds character, expands the mind and body, which all contributes to a successful and happy life. Jasper National Park.*

Left: W*hen normal people are sleeping at night, a mountain photographer is just beginning his work. Here on high, windswept Ptarmigan Peak (3059m) the author aims his camera towards the east. This 15-minute exposure, with the assistance of a large moon, created this mesmerizing image of nocturnal mystery. The lower foreground features Deception Pass (2475m); on the left stands Fossil Mountain (2946m). To the left on the horizon stands roundtopped Mt. Douglas (3235m); while on the right horizon looms rugged and taller Mt. St. Bride (3312m). Above it all is the blue firmament full of stars, galaxies, black holes, and who knows what else! Banff National Park.*

*A*nother serene and inspiring scene of autumnal Lower Consolation Lake when Larch trees turn gold. Soon the valley and the entire Rockies will retire for seven months of winter rest. On the horizon is Mt. Bell (2910m). A short walk southeast from Moraine Lake is very pleasant, exhilarating, and rewarding. The area is home to temperamental and unpredictable Grizzly Bear – caution is advised. Banff National Park.

*O*nly those who have been to Kananaskis country many times may appreciate this rare photo. Why? The place is windy, almost constantly, only very few days each year are calm. Luckily, the author was here on one of those rare days. The twin peaks of Mt. Kidd (2958m), one on the right is higher, catch first light on this chilly early summer morning. Snowy summits and morning mist lingering in the valley indicates that summer is not quite here yet.

Upper: R*emote, high and rugged The Royal Group stands tall west of the Palliser River as viewed from Mt. McHarg-Worthington massif of South Kananaskis. In the centre stands massive Mt. King George (3422m) flanked by Mt. Princess Mary on the left, Mt. Prince Albert on the right. An impressive mountain range.*

Lower: A *place of beauty and majesty – The Ramparts in Tonquin Valley – shines in a glorious autumn sunrise. The two Amethyst Lakes are fed by the Ramparts' snow and ice and give birth to Astoria River. This remote, high valley is home to numerous wildlife and rich flowery meadows and is viewed from Mt. Clitheroe. Jasper National Park.*

Left: M*t. Murchison (3333m) is a massive mountain comprised of seven towers over 3000m and is located north of the Mistaya River and east of the North Saskatchewan River. Reflected here in North Saskatchewan River, it was first ascended in 1902 by Collie, Stutfield and Week. Banff National Park.*

A major cataract on Kicking Horse River – the Wapta Falls is only a short hike away, one-hour return trip. The best time to view this spectacle is in early summer when water volumes are high. Mosquito spray is compulsory, bear spray optional. Late afternoon is the best light for photography. Yoho National Park.

A three-hour return invigorating hike gets one to Little Beehive from where a breathtaking view of Lake Louise and Fairview Mountain (2744m) provide a great reward. The trip may be combined with hiking up the Big Beehive from where the views are many and more spectacular. Banff National Park.

Above: M*t. Ball (3311m) is one giant of a mountain. It can hardly be seen from anywhere unless one takes a long hike. To see Mt. Ball, take Red Earth Creek trail to Shadow Lake, or from Radium Road to Ball Pass, or along Haffner Creek. The mountain is huge and difficult to ascend due to steep ice-covered walls on nearly all sides. This photo was taken from the ridge connecting Storm Mountain with Stanley Peak. Banff/Kootenay National Parks.*

Left: T*he northeast part of Lyell Icefield, four of five peaks of Mt. Lyell (3511m) and the ice that gives life to Arctomys Creek comprises this 25-year old vintage photo taken from Arctomys Peak (2792m). To get here take Glacier Lake trail to the end, then turn right and bushwack dense steep slopes of Arctomys to scree and the summit. The peak is not high but the location allows for splendid views of Lyell and Mons Icefields, the spectacular Forbes Group and its glaciers, and very picturesque, long Arctomys Creek Valley. Banff National Park.*

*O*riginating at the east margin of Wapta Icefield – Bow Glacier, the Bow River drains central Rockies and
is on its way to the bald Prairies of Alberta, as The Three Sisters (2936m) near Canmore look on.

Probably the most photographed mountain in the Canadian Rockies – Mt. Rundle (2998m) is located by the town of Banff and is reflected in First Vermilion Lake. The area still maintains a quite functional ecosystem, being so close to busy Banff.

Above: T*he different, 'unknown' image of Lake Louise. The glaciated landmark of Mt. Victoria is off the photo on the right. Here we see Fairview Mountain (2744m) flanking the lake on the south side. The early morning light, long shadows, the September chill, and a wide angle lens, make for a very pleasant image. Banff National Park.

Left: S*ome say that an entire pictorial book could be justified on this mesmerizing and incredible Valley of the Ten Peaks. Every season, almost every day brings a new mood, surprise and discovery. The complete list of 'Ten Peaks': Mt. Fay (3234m), Little (3140m), Bowlen (3072m), Tonsa (3054m), Perren (3051m), Allen (3310m), Tuzo (3245m), Deltaform (3424m), Neptuak (3237m),and Wenkchemna (3173m). Not all on photo. Banff National Park.

Above: Looking at Peyto Lake from the viewpoint, we see across the valley on left, lofty and rugged Caldron Peak (2917m). Quite easily climbed from the south, the author spent a relatively comfortable night here and the next sunny clear morning allowed for a photo of this interesting view to the south. From the left is Peyto Glacier, Peyto Peak, Caldron Lake and lofty icy giant – Mt. Baker looms on the horizon. Banff National Park.

Left: The same location as above, on the summit of Caldron Peak looking south along the ridge lit by rising sun. Peyto Glacier and Wapta Icefield in all its icy majesty. Ice, as dangerous as it is, presents the ultimate high mountain's feature. It is hard to accept that ice is melting at an incredible rate. It was always possible to ford Peyto Creek above the lake; now we face a large swift river. The higher the water level, the thinner the glacier – global warming can really be seen here, de facto.

Above: N*amed after an early explorer, guide and colourful character, Bill Peyto – Peyto Lake nestles in a quiet little valley just west of Bow Summit. The emerald waters originate from the Wapta Icefield and Peyto Glacier. The Lake's silty waters give birth to Mistaya River. Is that guy in the photo hiking or hitchhiking, or just giving a 'thumbs up' to affirm the beauty of this place. Banff National Park.*

Left: L*ate summer Fireweed adorn green and pristine Bow Lake as illuminated by morning sun. Crowfoot Mountain (3050m) looks on. Bow Lake depends on its emerald waters coming from Wapta Icefield just south of here. Too cold for fish but Moose love the area, spending the summers up here away from the nasty bugs. Banff National Park.*

Upper: A snow house or Igloo is a good alternative to a tent, only better. One need not tote a heavy tent – instead carry a shovel. Taking only one hour to build, an Igloo is warmer than a tent. When you 'close the door', the trapped air remains above freezing and your abode is completely quiet, no tent flaps to create noise. Eskimo (now Inuit) used Igloos for thousands of years and it worked very well for them. This luxurious snow house is on Bow Lake, richly illuminated with candles and a full moon. Banff National Park.

Lower: On the summit of Ptarmigan Peak (3059m) looking east, towards the sharp-jagged peaks of Sawback Range. Three distant peaks of Bonnet Peak (3235m) on the left viewed at sunrise. Banff National Park.

Upper: *T*hose were the days. Thirty years ago a young author took a younger friend and in a few hours they were in the midst of the Columbia Icefield. By the time they set up a shelter, a strong wind quickly developed into a full-fledged blizzard. The night was rough, fearsome and sleepless. The morning after, however, turned out to be absolutely spectacular. Here basking in the sun is Mt. Columbia (3747m), the second highest elevation in the Rockies, admired in September from the slopes of The Snow Dome. Jasper National Park.

Lower: *C*limbing Mt. Hector (3394m) rewards one with grand vistas virtually in all directions. Looking west at spectachlar Hector Lake and Waputik Icefield area at crisp September sunrise. Banff National Park.

Above: $\mathcal{B}$*ivouacking on the east slopes of Odaray Mtn. (3159m). High peaks of Bow Range line up the early night horizon. The pointy peak on the left is Mt. Huber, behind it is long ridge of Mt. Victoria, the white one at the centre is Mt. Lefroy, followed by Glacier and Ringrose Peaks. In the centre, famous emerald Lake O'Hara can be seen. Yoho National Park.*

Left: $\mathcal{H}$*ow many moons are there? Photographers often play with the nocturnal light and celestial occurrences. Here Herbert Lake near Lake Louise is the scene of multiple exposures of the moon which took circa four hours to complete. Seldom weather allows this kind of photo to succeed; any light breeze would spoil the reflections. Banff National Park.*

*P*uff, puff, puff! Yesteryears relived, nostalgia of the steamer era is recreated handsomely on Canada Day to the joy of all. Here is a jubilant little train whistling happily as it winds its way east along the Bow River near Lake Louise. This curve is named for Canadian Pacific staff photographer, Nick Morant, a man who consistently photographed trains with great passion his whole life long. Banff National Park.

*T*ower of Babel (2360m) on the left is a northern buttress of Mt. Babel, just east of Moraine Lake. The Tower looks small and inconspicuous but in reality this 300 metre high wall of fine quartzite is a major climbing site. The region east of Moraine Lake is quite lively and verdant; the Paintbrushes are tall and pretty, as are Poplars and Evergreens. West of here, high valleys support only limited flora and fauna. It is Larch tree country. Banff National Park.

*H*uge and roaring in the summer, Rearguard Falls on the Fraser River is little and quiet in October's dry season. This is the upper limit for spawning salmon. Supposedly a few may climb the falls and continue upstream only to encounter higher Overlander Falls, impossible to scale. West of Mt. Robson Park.

Mt. Christie (3103m) stands tall south of Athabasca River between Lick and Fryatt Creeks. Quite difficult to climb due to remote location and inhospitable topography. A little slough along Athabasca River provides mirror-like reflection on this crisp and gorgeous late October morning. Jasper National Park.

*M*t. Temple (3543m) is a well-known landmark by Lake Louise and ranks eleventh highest in the Rockies. The mountain is relatively easily accessible by trail from Moraine Lake – via Larch Valley. Before Sentinel Pass turn right into steep scree and continue to the summit. Sturdy hiking boots and being in good shape is all you need. To bivouac on the summit, as the author did a few times, requires more equipment, food and guts. On the left is Deltaform Mtn., Neptuak, then Weakchemna Pass. Right horizon is dominated by Mt. Goodsir (3562m); at right foreground stands Eiffel Peak and Tower. This icy and rocky paradise is viewed at crisp September sunrise. Banff National Park.

In 1898 two big-time explorers and climbers, J.N. Collie and H. Woolley, set foot for the first time on the summit of lofty Mt. Athabasca (3490m). From here the men discovered a vast icy desert – the Columbia Icefield. Because of highway proximity, the mountain is now a popular climbing site by many routes of various difficulties. Going straight up the icy north face is great fun. Any route one takes involves ice and crevasses and thus requires proper gear; going alone is strongly discouraged. After climbing this icy giant several times, including winter ascent, the author could not resist one more climb in 1998 to celebrate the 100th anniversary of the first ascent. Jasper National Park.

Above: Neither the photo nor the mountain is of any significance, but the idea behind it is. This is Mt. Terry Fox, just west of Mt. Robson, B.C. In 1980, young bone cancer stricken Terry Fox embarked on a gallant "Marathon of Hope". Starting at the Atlantic Ocean, he ran west towards the Pacific, roughly 42 kilometres a day. Completing more than half the distance, the cancer spread rapidly, terminating his heroic run. He raised millions for cancer research and immortalized himself. A few years later, another one-legged cancer victim, Steve Fonyo, ran the same way completing his Marathon at the Pacific coast, raising millions of dollars. These are the real great heroes, who have deeply touched the hearts of people around the world.

Left: This is the Athabasca River in the vicinity of Mt. Fryatt (at centre) in Jasper National Park, photographed in late October. In mid summer the water level is circa one meter higher. The river originates high at the Columbia Glacier of Columbia Icefield and drains northeastern slopes on its way north to join Peace, Slave and Mackenzie Rivers, to end its long journey at the Arctic Ocean. Bon voyage great river.

Above: October is freze-up time at Vermilion Lakes. Some corners of the lakes stay open, having little bubling mineral hot springs. Mt. Rundle (2998m) catches the last warm rays of the setting sun as winter is around the corner. Banff National Park.

Left: Countless stars "Circle" around the North Star or Polaris high above Castle Mountain (2766 m) as one little meteorite aims at the Tower, but misses by... a few million kilometres, The photo was exposed for one hour and 15 minutes on a quiet clear autumn night. Banff National Park.

The Larch Valley is one of those "must see" places which should be visited more than once. Every September when Larch Trees turn yellow-gold, thousands of people visit the valley nestled high above Moraine Lake. Come October when strong wind, combined with low temperatures, shakes the brown needles off and the high valley awaits the long, harsh winter. Glaciated and flamboyant Mt. Fay (3234m) shines in late afternoon sun under great blue Alberta skies. Banff National Park.

*P*robably seventy-five percent of the time Mt. Robson (3954m) is not visible, shrouded by heavy clouds. Being the highest in the Rockies, the monarch attracts all travelling by clouds and it rains 'cats and dogs' here with great benefit to flora and fauna. The mountain attracts many climbers and explorers but very few set their feet on this lofty and dangerous summit, defeated mostly by....the weather. Weather changes here so quickly that a sunny morning can become rainy and stormy two hours later.

Majestic Maligne Lake is a short drive southeast of Jasper. The scenic drive takes one along Medicine Lake to a high valley where the glacial lake nestles amidst stark ice-capped peaks. Charlton-Unwin Massif shines in late setting autumn sun. Jasper National Park.

*U*pper Waterfowl Lake is a summer home for Moose and several species of waterfowl. The shallow lake produces aquatic plants for wildlife, but if one came here in September the lake may already be frozen. On the left is Howse Peak (3290m) and Mt. Chephren (3266m). Banff National Park.

Forest fire is only seemingly destructive and disastrous. In reality it is a blessing when an old or sickly forest burns down. The soil is enriched by ashes; sunlight comes in allowing new trees and scores of plants to flourish, greatly benefitting flora and fauna. In 25 years a great new healthy forest will emerge. It is hard to know exactly how many fires are caused by lightning as opposed to human activities. It is certain careless smokers cause many fires and billions of dollar losses to the country's economy. Banning senseless smoking entirely seems to be the only logical and rational alternative. That would not only prevent 43,000 Canadians succumbing to cancer yearly, but would also save billions of health care dollars. In addition, millions of hectares of healthy forest would not be burned.

For millions of years the Rockies were affected only by natural forces like climatic changes, glaciation, erosion, earthquake, etc. Then humans appeared on the scene in increasing numbers. Over the last several decades, which witnessed rapid population explosion, the whole planet has been increasingly affected in negative, destructive ways.

We have simply run out of living space; quality of life deteriorates quickly as the world's population increases by 225,000 souls a day. Would you like to live in Tokyo with 27 million people, or Bombay 22 million, or Mexico City 20 million?

Desperate masses of humanity cut down trees to cook a meal, little realizing that soon the trees will be gone. Without trees and vegetation, life cannot be sustained. We are now talking about sustainable development. Given the present overpopulation and overdevelopment, the only rational direction to take is no development at all, and reducing population growth drastically is imperative.

More production and consumption only means faster and greater environmental degradation. Presently the world community facing rapidly increasing global warming, greenhouse gas, and ever-growing toxic emissions, tries to come to some solutions to slow down, reduce or somehow stop all the dangerous pollution we are producing.

Most of the world supports these efforts but a few industrial countries are engaging in verbal gymnastics, proposing their own solutions or wanting to go very slowly with any reduction of toxic emissions. It is clear these countries do not intend to reduce anything if it might harm their economies and profits. They must grow, produce, consume more, and thus generate more pollution. No one can produce and consume more and more, and cause less pollution. It is just not possible.

So what purpose does it serve to gain another few million dollars when the water you drink, the air you breathe, the food you consume, is so polluted that sooner or later, it will cause some deadly illness or disease that will kill you?

In the last 50 years, the world's nature has been more devastated than in the past thousand years. The wilderness is crumbling under heavy pressure of development, human activities and global pollution. Increasing road and railway traffic kills thousands of animals every year. In some areas, certain wildlife species, plants and flowers are extinct, where they were plentiful only 25 years ago. Damage is being inflicted by people because of ignorance. Some people believe the time is coming when, in order to enter a National or Wilderness Park, people will have to take a 'do's and don'ts' wilderness course.

How do you deal with people who pull up a plant or flower with the roots, smell and 'admire it', then drop it? And what about a vehicle which will carve a 'new road' in the pristine meadows, or people who collect and remove all they can find in a National Park? Yes, there are many people world-over who do just that. Their ignorance will destroy nature if they are not educated or prosecuted now. National Parks are designed to protect the pristine wilderness from development and abuse by uncaring people. Please remember that people are only visitors in National Parks. The permanent residents are the animals – it is their home and we must respect that. This is not only the law, but also the only logical way of behaviour. Get involved, react, let's save whatever is left of our green world. Look at and enjoy the pages of this edition; the Rockies are still stunningly beautiful. We must keep them that way forever, and you certainly can help.

THE AUTHOR

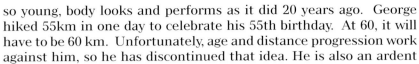

The prolific and enthusiastic author, George Brybycin, is a mountain man who has persistently photographed the Rockies for over 30 years and, as always, with love, passion and total devotion. His efforts produced 33 books, small and large, some good, some not so good, plain and controversial, but usually interesting, inspiring and attractive. His books always promote wholesome causes, educate and inform, even provoke and raise awareness of 'this and that', which some people may misconstrue, take the wrong way, or simply not understand George's rather complex mentality. George will never compromise or jeopardize his strong principles in order to gain a few pennies.

Right and wrong are clearly defined, no gray areas, in his analytical mind, which guides his life and work ethics. George's mountain activities and his publications have influenced and encouraged two generations of young mountain enthusiasts. His age could allow the Polish born author to slow down somewhat, especially after climbing 400 mountains. Instead, George just heads in the opposite direction. He climbs, photographs and publishes more than ever before. He takes credit for photographing all 51 mountains over 11000 ft./3353 m. in the Rockies, except for two.

Where does all that zest and energy come from, you may wonder. It has something to do with his lifestyle. George lives in the Rockies, breathes clean air and drinks pure water. He is a vegetarian, never smokes, drinks, or uses or abuses any substance. A good sense of humour and easy-going, jovial disposition, also help. So far his, not so young, body looks and performs as it did 20 years ago. George hiked 55km in one day to celebrate his 55th birthday. At 60, it will have to be 60 km. Unfortunately, age and distance progression work against him, so he has discontinued that idea. He is also an ardent traveller, explorer and adventurer. To date he has visited 36 countries, some many times.

George may be around for a while; however, recently he was diagnosed with a serous, supposedly incurable illness, known as workoholism (Labora laborus). Learning from nature and lofty mountains, George realized a long time ago how small and frail we humans are compared to nature's powerful forces, which have humbled him time and again. Nature's dazzling and gentle beauty formed George's mental make-up at an early age and remains deeply entrenched in his heart and soul.

George's publishing endeavours exclude the idea of profit or a 'get-rich' concept. He sells his books slightly above cost, to make them accessible to all. He lives happily at near poverty level by popular standards. For him, however, this represents a rich, fulfilling, purposeful life. When he saves a few extra dollars, he donates them to plant trees to help green up our increasingly gray, polluted world. To date, he has planted over 3000 trees. He tries to turn our envirnment a shade greener. 'To be or not to be' is not George's question: he knows exactly where he is going and how to get there. In his life and publications, he promotes a wholesome philosophy - beautiful ideas, truth, honesty, noble ideals, and a healthy, productive lifestyle.

Page 1 Vicinity of Lake O'Hara
Page 2 Shield Fern (Dryopteris)
Page 4 Lake Louise from Fairview Mtn.
Page 5 Painted Lady Butterfly
Page 6 Bighorn Sheep-Lamb
Page 7 Bunch Berry (Cornus Canadensis)
Page 15 Wild Botanical Garden

Front Cover: The Valley of the Ten Peaks
Back Cover: Rocky Mountain Monarch-Mt. Robson

This book was created in Alberta by Albertans
Printed in China by Everbest Printing Co.
Text Editor: Helen Turgeon
Design: George Brybycin
Typeseting: K & H United Co.
Colour Separations: Precision Colour Imaging
First Edition: 2003 Hard Cover
Copyright © 2003 by GB Publishing
All rights reserved
No parts of this book may be reproduced in any form
without written permission from the publisher,
except for brief passages quoted by a reviewer.

ISBN 0-919029-34-5

This is George Brybycin's 33rd book.

For current list, please write to:

GB PUBLISHING, Box 6292, Station D,
Calgary, Alberta Canada T2P 2C9

George Brybycin's collection of 15,000 35mm colour slides is FOR SALE at nominal price.
Subjects include: The Rockies, Western and Northern Canada, Calgary, The 1988 Olympics, Alaska, The Western U.S. and the World (Paris, London). Also available is the collection of all 33 George's books. Offers may be tendered to GB Publishing at the address above.